THE ART OF SUCCESS

How Extraordinary Artists Can Help You Succeed in Business and Life

Book Two: Coco Chanel

Cassandra Gaisford, BCA, Dip Psych

Cover by Cassandra Gaisford
Stock Photo: Shutterstock

Published by Blue Giraffe Publishing 2017
Blue Giraffe Publishing is a division of Worklife Solutions Ltd.
www.worklifesolutions.nz

For orders, please email: info@worklifesolutions.co.nz

See our complete catalogue at:
www.worklifesolutions.nz and
www.cassandragaisford.com

ISBN 978-0-9941314-8-5

First Edition

This book is dedicated to love

FREE WORKBOOK!

Thank you for your interest in my new book *The Art of Success.* I've listened to feedback from my readers who told me they were short on time but high on motivation, so I've kept this one deliberately short.

If you'd like a longer book to help you follow your passion to success I'm excited to be giving you another book for FREE! You'll also be subscribed to my newsletter where I share inspirational tips and strategies to help you succeed.

Follow this link to subscribe and download the free *Find Your Passion Workbook*

http://worklifesolutions.leadpages.co/free-find-your-passion-workbook

I hope you enjoy it

A simple life, with a husband and children—a life with people you love—that is the real life

~ Coco Chanel

CONTENTS

FOREWORD..13

AUTHOR'S NOTE 15

HOW TO USE THIS BOOK..23

PRINCIPLE ONE: THE CALL FOR SUCCESS 29

WHAT IS SUCCESS? 31

FOLLOW YOUR PASSION 33

REALITY CHECK 35

BARKING UP THE WRONG TREE 37

REALIZE YOUR POTENTIAL 39

LIVE AND WORK WITH PURPOSE............................ 41

PRINCIPLE TWO: EMPOWER YOUR SUCCESS 43

DREAM BIG 45

PERFUME YOUR LIFE 48

YOUR SUCCESS NUMBERS 50

STAY SPARKLY..53

DRESS JOYFULLY 56

KEEP LEARNING.. 58

PRINCIPLE THREE: EMPOWER YOUR VISION.............61

STAY TRUE TO YOUR VISION 63

AWAKEN THE SEER... 66

REINVENT YOUR LIFE 68

BOOST YOUR MOTIVATION...71

MASTER THE ELEMENTAL ART OF SIMPLICITY....75

MAKE A PASSION ACTION PLAN 77

AFFIRM THAT YOU DESERVE SUCCESS.................. 80

PRINCIPLE FOUR: EMPOWER YOUR SPIRIT 83

SELF-RELIANCE 85

BELONG TO YOURSELF..87

GET CREATIVE.. 89

CHANGE YOUR NAME 92

PRAY... 95

MAINTAIN YOUR FAITH... 98

CONSULT THE ORACLES... 95

PRINCIPLE FIVE: EMPOWER YOUR MIND..................107

FAITH IN YOUR STARS 109

BOOST YOUR SELF-AWARENESS 113

CREATE A NEW LIFE STORY 116

ACCENT THE POSITIVE................................119

FAILURE IS NOT FATAL 121

MAKE MISTAKES 124

BOOST YOUR BELIEF 128

PRINCIPLE SIX: EMPOWER YOUR BODY....................133

SHARPEN YOUR MOST POTENT TOOL WITH SCENT
....135

RESTORE YOUR ENERGY............................. 137

SURROUND YOURSELF WITH NATURE..................141

WALK!...144

HEALTHY SPIRITUAL SIGNIFICANCE 133

YOUR BODY BAROMETER............................. 135

PRINCIPLE SEVEN: EMPOWER YOUR
RELATIONSHIPS.. 151

MAINTAIN YOUR INDEPENDENCE 153

LIVE WITH OTHERS 155

FLEE FALSE LOVE.......................................143

HEAL YOUR WOUNDS...................................145

LET THE CHILDREN PLAY 147

CONFLICT HAPPENS....................................149

SHOW YOUR STRENGTH................................ 151

PRINCIPLE EIGHT: EMPOWER YOUR WORK 155

BE A LOVE MARK 157

FOLLOW YOUR JOY 160

DO THE WORK...164

TAKE YOUR CHANCE....................................167

BE ORIGINAL 169

KNOW WHEN TO CHANGE 171

JEALOUS SABOTEURS.................................. 171

GIVE GENEROUSLY.....................................176

CONCLUSION: BEAUTY AND THE BEST 195

THE TRUTH ABOUT SUCCESS.........................198

FURTHER RESOURCES...................................207

GRATITUDES 211

ABOUT THE AUTHOR....................................215

FOREWORD

As the opening of this book promises, if you're short on time but high on motivation, then this is the book that can help you move toward your success.

It's amazing how much can be packed into a book that can be read in one sitting. But if you do, be prepared to come back to the *Art of Success* again and again because there is not only wisdom on every page, but actionable, immediate steps you can take to make a difference in reaching your own goals and dreams.

This book is like meeting with your best friend—the one who can give you a pep talk or a sharp rap on the head, depending on what you need.

Broken into small, bite-sized segments—you'll soon find yourself jotting notes down, finding someone else to share the insights and experience with, and even more resources made available to keep you motivated and focused.

Power-packed is the word that came to mind as I was reading, nodding and inspired. Cassandra Gaisford created a real gem in what I have no doubt will be a life-changing series for many people. Don't just take my word for it. Keep reading!

—Mary Buckham, USA Today Best Selling Author
and International Writing Craft Instructor

AUTHOR'S NOTE

Those on whom legends
are built are their legends

~ Lisa Chaney, biographer

Gabrielle Bonheur "Coco" Chanel had to overcome obstacles to success just like you and I. She suffered many hardships, including the death of her mother when she was young, being abandoned by a father who didn't love her, growing up in an orphanage, and the stigma of her early years which plagued her throughout her life.

She suffered extreme poverty, self-doubt, low self-esteem and craved love. People jealous of her talent also spread malicious rumors and tried to undermine her success.

But she didn't let obstacles stop her from doing the work she loved. The pursuit of excellence born from her experience, fueled by her determination to be an independent woman, and the desire to liberate others, ultimately led to her success.

Her boundless imagination, strength of purpose and courageous spirit is an inspiration to young and old.

I created *The Art of Success* series to reveal how the success secrets and strategies of extraordinary artists like Coco Chanel can help people like you and I succeed—personally and professionally.

Successful artists have always struggled, but they persevered anyway. And it is this willingness to pursue their calling in the face of many challenges that holds lessons for us all.

Who Is This Book For?

If you want to challenge conventional definitions of success and live a life on your own terms, this book is for you.

If you're an aspiring creative, or an accomplished one, *The Art of Success* will provide support and encouragement to continue the journey.

If you suffer from fear, doubt, procrastination, or overly seek validation from others, *The Art of Success* will come to your rescue.

If you're a Type A personality looking for the fastest route to success, *The Art of Success* will challenge you to experiment with going quickly slowly, to avoid burning out. Or overrunning the turn-off that would lead you down the path less travelled—the route that may lead you to your most enduring success.

Or you might, like me, be passionate about Coco Chanel and all that she achieved, and want to discover her success secrets.

Your Concise Guide to Success

The Art of Success is a concise guide to succeeding in business and in life. My vision was simple: a few short, easy to digest tips for time-challenged people who were looking for inspiration and practical strategies to encourage positive change.

I knew that people didn't need a wad of words to feel inspired, gain clarity and be stimulated to take action.

In coaching and counseling sessions I'd encourage my clients to ask a question they would like answered. The questions could be specific, such as, 'How can I make a living from my passion?' Or vague, for example, 'What do I most need to know?' They were always amazed at how readily answers flowed.

In this era of information obesity, the need for simple, life-affirming messages is even more important. If you are looking for inspiration and practical tips, in short, sweet sound bites, this guide is for you.

Similarly, if you are a grazer, or someone more methodical, this guide will also work for you. Pick a section or page at random, or work through the principles sequentially. I encourage you to experiment, be open-minded and try new things. I promise you will achieve outstanding results.

Let experience be your guide, as it was Coco's. Give your brain a well-needed break. Let go of 'why' and embrace how you feel or how you want to feel. Honor the messages from your intuition and follow your path with heart.

At the time of writing I've just turned to 'Principle Three: Invent Your Life'. It's a timely reminder that I can transcend the things I dislike and create a life that fills me with joy—no matter what seemingly insurmountable obstacles block my path. The following remark from Coco may also speak to you: "I invented my life by taking for granted that everything I did not like would have an opposite, which I would like."

How This Book Will Help You

Whenever I'm in a slump or needing an inspirational boost, I turn to people who are smarter or more skilled than me for good advice.

I've done the same with qualities I've wanted to develop, like patience. "What would Mother Theresa do now?" I asked myself many years ago. Mother Theresa wouldn't shout! She wouldn't lose her cool. She'd send loving kindness and smile. And that's what I did whenever I got frustrated.

Coco Chanel was super smart! As I wrote *The Art of Success*, I applied the strategies I'm sharing with you in my own life—personally and professionally.

If you've been procrastinating, experiencing self-doubt, feeling fearful, or just getting in your own way, you're in good company. Coco's been there. I've been there too—as have many successful people. Guess what, getting in your own way is normal!

I promise there are solutions to the problems you're currently facing—and you'll find them in the pages that follow.

Dig into this book and let Coco Chanel be your mentor, inspiration and guide as she calls forth your passions, purpose and potential.

Through the teachings of Coco, extensive research into the mysteries of motivation, success and fulfillment, and my own personal experience and professional success with clients as an holistic psychologist, *The Art of Success* will help you accelerate success. Together, Coco and I will guide you to where you need to go next, and give you practical steps to achieve success.

I was once told that I had the soul of an artist. Actively discouraged in childhood, for a long time I'd closed off that side of me. I began my career as a bank-teller, then as an accountant, then as a recruitment consultant, followed by more 'business-minded' careers. I even spent time in prison—on a work assignment.

Each time I went further and further away from who I truly was and the things that gave me joy. Like Coco Chanel, I wasn't encouraged to pursue my natural inclination. My hope is that after reading *The Art of Success* you will be!

Whether your calling is the world of fashion, commerce, or seeking answers in the stars, it's never too late to be yourself.

Step into this ride joyfully and start creating your best life today.

HOW TO USE THIS BOOK

In the first book of *The Art of Success* series, I shared how Leonardo da Vinci was a systems thinker who recognized and valued the interconnectedness of everything. He can teach us many lessons, including the link between passion and inspiration, mental strength, emotional resilience, spiritual power, health and well-being, empowering relationships, smart goals and authentic success.

The *Art of Success* takes a holistic look at what it means, and what it takes, to be successful.

The Eight Principles of Success

I've sectioned *The Art of Success* into a cluster of principles. Principles aren't constricting rules unable to be shaped, but general and fundamental truths which may be used to help guide your choices.

Let's look briefly at The Eight Principles of Success and what each will cover:

Principle One, "The Call For Success" will help you explore the truth about success and define success on your own terms. You'll discover the rewards and 'realities' of success, and intensify success-building beliefs.

Principle Two, "Empower Your Success," will help you learn why igniting the fire within, love, and heeding the call for passion is the cornerstone of future success. You'll clarify who you really are and who you want to be, discover your elemental, signature strengths, and clarify your passion criteria.

Sight was the sense Leonardo valued above all else. **Principle Three, "Empower Your Vision,"** will help you clarify and visualize what you really want to achieve. You'll then be better able to decide where best to invest your time and energy. You'll also begin exploring ways to develop your life and career in light of your passions and life purpose, maintain focus and bring your vision into successful reality.

Principle Four, "Empower Your Spirit," urges you to pay attention to the things that feed your soul, awaken your curiosity, stir your imagination and create passion in your life.

Principle Five, "Empower Your Mind," looks at ways to cultivate a success mindset. You'll also identify strategies to overcome obstacles and to maximize your success, and ways to work less but achieve more to gain greater balance and fulfillment.

Your health is your wealth yet it's often a neglected part of success. **Principle Six, "Empower Your Body,"** recognizes the importance of a strong, flexible and healthy body to your mental, emotional, physical and spiritual success. You'll be reminded of simple strategies which reinforce the importance of quality of breath, movement, nutrition and sleep. Avoiding burnout is also a huge factor in attaining success. When you do less, and look after yourself more, you can and will achieve success.

Principle Seven, "Empower Your Relationships" will help you boost your awareness of how surrounding yourself with your vibe tribe will fast track your success, and when it's best to go it alone.

The Art of Success ends with **Principle Eight, "Empower Your Work"** and emphasizes the role of authenticity and being who you are. You'll also learn how to 'fake it until you make it' and be inspired by others' successes. Importantly you'll learn how following your own truth will set you free.

How to Best Enjoy This Book

Think of *The Art of Success* like a shot of espresso. Sometimes one quick hit is all it takes to get started. Sometimes you need a few shots to sustain your energy. Or maybe you need a bigger motivational hit and then you're on your way.

You're in control of what works best for you. Go at your own pace, but resist over-caffeinating. A little bit of guidance here-and-there can do as much to fast track your success as consuming all the principles in one hit.

Skim to sections that are most relevant to you, and return to familiar ground to reinforce home truths. But most of all enjoy your experience.

Your Challenge

"I love your works to date—provocative and supportive at the same time," a gentleman who'd read my *Mid-Life Career Rescue* books wrote to me recently.

To provoke is to incite or stimulate. It's the reason I've included open-ended questions and calls to action in each guide. The best questions are open, generative ones that don't allow for 'yes/no' answers; rather they encourage you to tap into your higher wisdom, intuition, or go in search of answers—as both Coco and Leonardo did.

Dive Deeper with *The Art of Success* Workbook

The Art of Success print book will also be available as a workbook, with space to write your responses to the challenges and calls to action within the book.

Expand Your Learning—Follow My Blog

Dive deeper into some of the insights I've shared and signup to my newsletter and follow my blog—navigate to here www.cassandragaisford.com

Inspirational Quotes to Support and Empower

Sometimes all it takes is one encouraging word, one timely bit of advice to awaken your power within. Throughout *The Art of Success* I've balanced Chanel's wisdom with other feminine and masculine strength—

choosing from a wide range of super-capable men and women, historical and current, young and old.

They are men and women who shared Coco's interests and also had to overcome significant obstacles on the way to success.

Be Empowered

Empowerment is defined as giving power or authority to someone or something—who better to decide who assumes this power and sovereign authority than you.

Empowered people do what they need to do to assume mastery over their thoughts, feelings, emotions and things that affect their lives.

Empowered people are successful people because they live life on their terms. They do the things that really matter to them and those they love.

Empowered people are resilient in the face of setbacks, disappointments or attacks and they're flexible enough to tackle obstacles in their path.

Like Coco Chanel, they recognize they are the experts and sovereign authority in their lives. They learn from, and surround themselves with other empowered successful people. They back themselves even when they don't succeed.

Are you ready to heed the call for success, and define success on your own terms?

Let's get started!

PRINCIPLE ONE:

THE CALL FOR SUCCESS

WHAT IS SUCCESS?

*There are people who have money
and people who are rich*

~ Coco Chanel

Success is hard to define but easy to see and feel when you have achieved it. Being successful isn't necessarily about how much money you have, how many homes you own, or any of the other things people obsessed with material possessions covet.

Being successful for increasing numbers of people includes: maintaining good health, energy and enthusiasm for life, fulfilling relationships, creative freedom, well-being, peace of mind, happiness and joy. Success also includes the ability to achieve your desires, whatever these may be, and being true to yourself.

Coco Chanel once said, "How many cares one loses when one decides not to be something but to be someone."

When you commit to being the creator of your life, and defining success on your own terms, you choose your '*someone.*' You will create and narrate the story of your life—just as Coco did.

Your Challenge

What does success mean to you?

How will you know when you have succeeded?

Who are you, or will you become?

What will the first line be in the story of your life?

The privilege of a lifetime is being who you are

~ Joseph Campbell, author

FOLLOW YOUR PASSION

Passion goes. Boredom remains

~ Coco Chanel

Coco Chanel's extraordinarily passionate nature, and her ambitious quest for success, drove and sustained her throughout her life and career.

She once said, "In order to be irreplaceable, one must always be different." This is where following your soul's code, and living and working with passion comes in.

Passion is a source of huge spiritual energy which enables you to produce extraordinary results. Remarkable people get noticed and find life interesting. Passion:

- Helps people lead bigger lives
- Is an indispensable part of success
- Helps people achieve
- Energizes
- Liberates
- Allows people to be themselves

- Leads you to new opportunities and fresh horizons

- Boosts health and longevity

Your Challenge

What will passion do for you?

Be passionate even if people think you're crazy

If you need more help finding and living your passion, my book *Find Your Passion and Purpose: Four Easy Steps to Discover a Job You Want and Live the Life You Love* will help. Available as a paperback and eBook from Amazon—navigate to here getBook.at/Passion

My intuition, my intention and my passion have allowed me to be who I am and will take me to higher ground

~ Oprah Winfrey, businesswoman

REALITY CHECK

*Success is often achieved by those who
don't know that failure is inevitable*

~ Coco Chanel

Pursuing and sustaining passion-driven success is not always fun. Like anything worthwhile, following your passion often involves great commitment, hard work and sacrifice.

Passionate people are prepared to give up things to live a more interesting life—Netflix, lounging on the sofa and indulging in a life of excess are just some of things that come to mind.

Passionate people are prepared to take risks and cope with failure. But the compensation is a bigger, fuller, more significant life filled with drive and purpose.

Your Challenge

What are you prepared to trade-off to be more passionate?

What are you willing to change in your life? What would stop you?

What, or who, could inspire and sustain your quest for success?

I have learned throughout my life as a composer chiefly through my mistakes and pursuits of false assumptions, not by my exposure to founts of wisdom and knowledge

~ Igor Stravinsky, composer

BARKING UP THE WRONG TREE

Luxury must be comfortable,
otherwise it is not luxury

~ Coco Chanel

Are you chasing the right dream? The ultimate luxury many people say, including Coco, is to become who and what you really desire. But many people trade off their deeper passions for material comforts and status that can only ever give fleeting satisfaction.

Others lose their sense of self, trade their integrity, smother their personality, and set fire to their relationships, chasing success at all costs.

Coco Chanel once said that one of her biggest regrets is that she didn't spend more time devoting herself to love—instead she chased the wrong dream.

Outwardly, people barking up the wrong tree appear successful but in fact they are deeply unfulfilled. As Coco Chanel once said, "A simple life, with a husband and children—a life with people you love—that is the real life." It's something she never achieved.

Your Challenge

Are you chasing the right dream?

When you achieve success, will you be happy with the person you've become?

Will any sacrifices you've made be worth it?

Are you ready for the day that we've prayed for? Already holding what is real You know the soul finds its own evolution. And this is the only love I feel. And I tell you I'm keeping up the strength. I've gotta try

~ Barbara Streisand, singing 'Come Tomorrow'

REALIZE YOUR POTENTIAL

*In order to be irreplaceable
one must always be different*

~ Coco Chanel

A life of no regret—isn't that what we all want? In my professional practice as a holistic psychologist and career coach, so many people have told me they wished they had followed their passion and seized opportunities earlier, but that they lacked the courage to follow their convictions.

Often, they wait to be pushed before they make the leap toward realizing their potential. Abraham Maslow theorized in his hierarchy of needs model that becoming a self-actualized person was the driving ambition and purpose of life. The ultimate success, he claimed, was to be all that you are capable of becoming.

Mademoiselle Coco Chanel threw herself into this quest with audacious determination. She vowed not to settle for the life into which she was born.

Instead she devoted herself to realizing her potential. With ferocious willpower, she aligned with the people who could elevate her success. How else could an impoverished orphan defy her origins and soar to eternal glory? To fulfill her potential Coco Chanel continually reinvented herself. She knew that success equaled growth, aligning with her heart's desire, and taking inspired action.

Being true to yourself, and honoring the passion of your soul, can be the most beautiful feeling of all.

Your Challenge

Are you ready to reinvent your life and achieve your greatest potential? Or are you too comfortable? Are you stagnating, not growing, nor challenging or exciting yourself? Don't settle for okay

Perhaps it's the fear of the unknown, or starting over, failing or succeeding. Fear is part of the human condition. It reminds you you're alive. It doesn't have to stop you from succeeding. How could gaining more self-mastery benefit your life and boost your success?

You must learn to follow your destiny, whatever it maybe, with joy. As flowers grow they show off their beauty and are appreciated by all; then, after they die, they leave their seeds so that others may continue God's work

~ Paulo Coelho, author in his book, *The Spy*

LIVE AND WORK WITH PURPOSE

Fashion has two purposes: comfort and love. Beauty comes when fashion succeeds

~ Coco Chanel

Coco built a career on refashioning women's ideas of themselves. Liberating women from the confines of restrictive corsets, and socially sanctioned norms about what was acceptable attire, gave her a definitive life purpose. Her life's mission was to create more love, beauty and joy in women's lives and in those who loved them.

Everything she committed to achieve was done with purpose.

Given that you spend so much of your life working, and you're living longer too, it's even more important to pursue your calling. Do you still need convincing?

Benefits of working and living with purpose include:

✓ Giving you an edge, firing the flames of passion, enthusiasm, drive and initiative needed to succeed

✓ The courage, tenacity and clarity of vision needed to thrive

✓ Fueling the embers of flagging motivation and empowering latent dreams

✓ Leading you to the work you were born to do

✓ Discovering your true calling opens you up to the dreams the Universe has for you—bigger than you can dream for yourself.

Your Challenge

What life experiences give you meaning and purpose?

How could your purpose benefit you and others?

It is in giving that I connect with others, with the world and with the divine

~ Isabel Allende, author

PRINCIPLE TWO:

EMPOWER YOUR SUCCESS

DREAM BIG

I invented my life by taking for granted that everything I did not like would have an opposite, which I would like

~ Coco Chanel

In the movie, '*The Pursuit of Happyness*,' Will Smith, who plays the role of a homeless man, says to his son, "You got a dream, you gotta protect it. People can't do something themselves, they wanna tell you that you can't do it. You want something? Go get it. Period."

As a child, Coco dreamed big. The flames of her desires were in part fueled by reading romance novels full of dashing heroes and heroines living absurdly, audaciously opulent and liberated lives.

I'm sure plenty of people tried to sabotage Coco's dreams of success—but she dreamed big dreams anyway. She knew that reality was a matter of perception, and once said that she would pretend she didn't hear people who criticized her, and could not see people with whom she disagreed.

Her strong will, boundless imagination, strength of purpose and courageous spirit are an inspiration to young and old.

People who are impatient to see the realization of your dreams may say, "Show me the money" or "You've left it too late," or some other 'downer' message.

Ignore them.

"It's already been done," people said to Tim Ferris when he shared his idea of starting a podcast. Instead of letting others talk him out of starting his show, he did it anyway.

His podcast is now ranked #1 business podcast on all of iTunes. It is the first business/interview podcast to pass 100,000,000 downloads. It was also selected as iTunes' "Best of 2014," "Best of 2015" and "Best of 2016". Tim Ferris has also been called "the Oprah of radio".

Your Challenge

Dream big. Everything starts as someone's daydream

Fuel your verve—pursue the vision that sparkles

Become audaciously obsessed

Dream big but plan small. Baby steps will lead to bigger success

Anchor your dreams within your heart and feel as though they are already achieved

Create a soundtrack to feed your dreams. I still love Miley Cyrus's, *The Climb*, particularly the encouraging lyrics to persist and persevere.

"Ain't about how fast I get there. Ain't about what's waiting on the other side It's the climb."

Remember, you go where your vision is. Think big, feel big, and know in your heart that you are one with God, and you will project a radiance, a glow, a confidence, a joy, and a healing vibration which bless all who come within your orbit now and forevermore

~ Joseph Murphy, PhD, author and New Thought minister

PERFUME YOUR LIFE

A woman who doesn't wear perfume has no future

~ Coco Chanel

After the death of her playboy lover, Boy Chapel, Chanel became the mistress of the Russian Grand Duke Dmitri Pavlovich. Through him, she met Ernest Beaux, an expert perfumer whose father had worked for the Russian Czar.

Beaux was working on an essence for the French perfume maker Francois Coty. According to legend, after sampling the scent, Chanel made a few suggestions, then convinced Beaux to give it to her.

In 1924, she released it as Chanel N°5. It was the first perfume ever to bear a designer's name. She boldly advertised it as "A very improper perfume for nicely brought-up ladies."

The dark, leathery, distinctly masculine blend in its Art Deco bottle proved to be liquid gold.

With an uncanny knack of marketing nouse Coco quickly recognized the power of wooing Hollywood stars. When screen siren Marilyn Monroe was asked, "What do you wear to bed?" she famously answered,

"Why, Chanel N°5, of course." Coco's fortune was made.

The transcendent alchemy of the potions that went into this formula was not left to chance. Grieving after Boy Chapel's death, jasmine, ylang-ylang, vetiner and other restorative scents imbued Chanel N°5 with hope, healing, and the sensual confidence that love lost would be found again.

Aromatherapy, using the scents of plants and flowers, is one of many ancient remedies validated by modern science today. It's the Swiss army knife of all things healing—physically, mentally, spiritually and emotionally.

Your Challenge

Investigate the power of smell

What scents imbue you with confidence?

Create your own success blend, or have an expert create one for you. Beginning with how you want to feel is a good place to start

I live to succeed, not

to please you or anyone else

~ Marilyn Monroe, actress

YOUR SUCCESS NUMBERS

I'm presenting my dress collection on the 5th of May, the fifth month of the year

~ Coco Chanel

You may believe in lucky numbers or you may call it superstition but many clever minds, including Einstein, Leonardo da Vinci, and ancient philosophers, revered the science and sacred mysteries of numerology.

Coco Chanel believed so strongly in the power of the number five that she named her perfume Chanel N°5 after it. Chanel N°5 is still a world favorite nearly one hundred years after its conception.

She knew the numerological significance of the number five, as representative of the fifth element—the legendary *quinta essentia* of the alchemists: the classical quintessence of which the cosmos is made.

Coco's interest in the language and magic of numbers was also sparked during her time amongst the nuns.

At the age of twelve, Chanel was handed over to the care of nuns, and for the next six years spent a stark, disciplined existence in a convent orphanage, Aubazine, founded by Cistercians in the 12th century.

From her earliest days, the number five had potent associations for her. The paths that led Chanel to the cathedral for daily prayer were laid out in circular patterns repeating the number five.

Her affinity for the number five co-mingled with the abbey gardens, and by extension the lush surrounding hillsides abounding with cistus—a five-petal rose.

In 1920, when presented with small glass vials containing sample scent compositions numbered 1 to 5 and 20 to 24 for her assessment, she chose the fifth vial.

Chanel told her master perfumer, Ernest Beaux, whom she had commissioned to develop a fragrance with modern innovations: "I present my dress collections on the fifth of May, the fifth month of the year and so we will let this sample number five keep the name it has already, it will bring good luck."

For Coco, the number five was especially esteemed as signifying the pure embodiment of a thing, its spirit, its mystic meaning.

Along with brilliant minds like Leonardo da Vinci, she was guided by the sacredness of numbers and divine proportion. Some of the world's most enduring sacred monuments and successful brands dedicated to worship, beauty, and excellence have been inspired by a devotion to numbers.

Your Challenge

Look deeper into the world of numbers and proportion and discover their secret mysteries

What numbers are significant to you?

What numbers might herald your success?

Without mathematics there is no art

~ Fra Luca Bartolomeo de Pacoli , mathematician

Learn more about Leonardo da Vinci's success formula in the first book in, *The Art of Success: How Extraordinary Artists Can Help You Succeed in Business and Life (Book One: Leonardo da Vinci)*. Navigate to here—getBook.at/TheArtofSuccess

STAY SPARKLY

You can be gorgeous at thirty, charming at forty, and irresistible for the rest of your life

~ Coco Chanel

"Don't let anything dull your sparkle," writes psychologist and angel believer Doreen Virtue in her book of the same name.

Despite the darkness of her childhood Coco Chanel lived a very sparkly life. She used an eclectic array of strategies to maintain her sparkle, including designing and surrounding herself with things that gave her joy.

In her Parisian apartment a chandelier designed by Coco was adorned with dozens of crystal orbs and stars, camellias and grapes.

As Justine Picardie writes in her excellent book, *The Legend and The Life,* "Hidden letters and numbers in the black wrought-iron frame begin to emerge: G's for Gabrielle, Chanel's name at christening; double C's for Coco Chanel, the name under which she became famous; and fives—the number which made her a fortune, as the label on the perfume that still sells more than any other brand in the world."

To break free of negativity and drama Chanel would retreat to her beautiful apartment in the Ritz. There she would look at the symbols and reminders that provided meaning and sustained her—including simple white camellias that gave her so much joy.

The white camellia is rich with symbolism—it speaks to the heart and expresses positive feelings. It's most common meanings are:

- Adoration

- Refinement

- Perfection and excellence

- Faithfulness and longevity

These meanings were all very central to Coco's philosophy of life and career success.

Your Challenge

How can you break free of negativity and drama?

What, or who, can you surround yourself with to fill you with more joy?

How can you stay irresistible for the rest of your life?

What symbols reinforce what's most important to you?

*If you are unhappy with anything . . .
whatever brings you down, get rid of it.
When you are free, your true creativity,
your true self comes out*

~ Tina Turner, singer

DRESS JOYFULLY

. . . the grand problem, the most important problem, is to rejuvenate women.
To make women look young. Then their outlook changes. They feel more joyous

~ Coco Chanel

Coco was a trailblazer in women's fashion. When she arrived wearing trousers in Venice people were shocked. But shock quickly turned to awe. Women wanted what she had—and Coco was only too happy to sell it to them.

Her joyous color was black. She loved its simplicity and understated elegance. Perhaps it reminded her of the habits the nuns, who so tenderly cared for her, wore.

Whatever the catalyst was, Coco had the vision to turn black, the color of mourning, into the symbol of independence, freedom, and strength. She also created the now iconic little black dress!

Your joyous color may be yellow, blue, or gold. Or it may be multi-patterned and have all the colors of the rainbow. Floating dresses in the finest silk may instill you with confidence, or perhaps you prefer something more tailored.

Whatever your color, whatever you wear, be sure that it makes you feel joyful.

Your Challenge

Act as if. Take a job or lifestyle idea that you are considering, or have always wondered what it would be like, and act as if you are living that role. Dress the part

Have your 'colors' professionally confirmed by a trained image consultant—when you dress in the colors that suit your skin tone you'll look younger and feel fabulous

Dress shabbily and they remember the dress; dress impeccably and they remember the woman

~ Coco Chanel

KEEP LEARNING

I would make a very bad dead person, because once I was put under, I would grow restless and would think only of returning to earth and starting all over again

~ Coco Chanel

Maintaining a commitment to lifelong learning—gaining new knowledge and new skills—is an important component of success.

Many personal and business failures can be attributed to not keeping abreast of trends, failing to adapt to changing landscapes, and misguided complacency.

Whether you succeed or not is as much about your willingness to start from the beginning, shear a path through the unknown, and what you learn along the way—including what to do and what not to do.

But some people fear learning. They fear not being regarded as excellent in their field—*immediately.* Others fear being exposed as someone who doesn't have all the answers, making mistakes, and failing.

Coco Chanel wasn't born knowing how to be a hat designer, nor how to make clothes, nor how to run a business—especially in a terrain dominated by men.

Her commitment to acquiring knowledge, and willingness to learn from others, as well as her own trials and errors, led to her great accomplishments.

Learning through experience also led to some of her biggest lessons—many of which cost her dearly.

For example, with the benefit of hindsight she wished she'd never gone into partnership with Alain and Gerard Wertheimer to produce and distribute Chanel N°5.

Coco spent many years locked in an acrimonious battle to gain a fairer portion of the profits of the perfume she created.

Your Challenge

How can you embrace continual learning?

Who, or what, could be your greatest teacher?

How can you stay restless for new knowledge?

Learn to work harder on yourself than you do on your job. If you work hard on your job you can make a living, but if you work hard on yourself you'll make a fortune

~Jim Rohn, author

PRINCIPLE THREE:

EMPOWER YOUR VISION

STAY TRUE TO YOUR VISION

I wanted to give a woman comfortable clothes that would flow with her body. A woman is closest to being naked when she is well-dressed

~ Coco Chanel

As Adam Markel writes in his book, *Pivot: The Art and Science of Reinventing Your Career and Life,* "Just because you can't see the steps doesn't mean they aren't there. There's a word for this type of behavior. It's called faith." This faith is shaped by gaining clarity about your purpose in life.

Coco's vision, and her resultant success, was clearly fueled by a strong sense of purpose. She wanted to unbind women from their corsets, to free them from restrictions, to liberate them from bondage. And she did this by creating clothes that empowered.

Before embarking on your visionary journey, you need to let go of "The Plan," and needing to have concrete guarantees before taking your first steps. You also need to disconnect from your ego and connect to God source, Markel says.

No doubt this was in part how Coco achieved her success. The seeds were planted when she was born to a seamstress mother, and blossomed in the orphanage where she learned how to sew.

More steps unfolded when she was drawn by the wonderful costumes in a local cabaret, and first enchanted Etienne Balsan, the wealthy man who would become her benefactor, with her beauty and voice. She left Etienne for one of his wealthier friends, Arthur "Boy" Capel. Both men were instrumental in financing Coco's first fashion venture.

In 1910 she opened her first shop on Paris's *Rue Cambon.* Coco started out designing and selling hats. She later added stores in Deauville and Biarritz and began making clothes.

Her first taste of success came from a dress she fashioned on a damp dull day out of an old jersey. So many people asked her where she got the dress from that she offered to make one for them.

"My fortune is built on that old jersey that I'd put on because it was cold in Deauville," she once told author Paul Morand.

Further opportunities (and tragedies) unfolded, guiding her step-by-step toward her destiny. For example, she only encountered the perfume expert who would later make her famous, when she went on a retreat to grieve the tragic death of her lover.

Importantly, while she had a clear purpose guiding her vision, she was quick to act on opportunities as they presented.

Your Challenge

What are you clinging to that's preventing you from seeing your potential clearly?

How can you fortify your faith in your own vision, beliefs and goals—and stick to them?

Be your own cheerleader and do not wait for approval nor support from others, listen to your gut and go for it

Live your own truths and don't be challenged or coerced into conforming—it's all about your life path and rediscovering your power

Following your dreams is not always practical, but not impossible. Most are attainable to some degree.

It's always fantastic to feel that your vision is being pursued in some way and not buried and forgotten.

The only thing worse than being blind is having sight but no vision

~ Helen Keller, author

AWAKEN THE SEER

If you were born without wings, do nothing to prevent them from growing

~ Coco Chanel

Several years ago when I was in New York I stumbled on a book that was to change my life—*Psychic Living: Tap into Your Psychic Potential*, by Andrei Ridgeway.

"In this technological day and age filled with busywork," Ridgeway writes, "many of us neglect our psychic potential. Our instincts are repressed and our inner voices buried.

"For many people the word 'psychic' is so titanic, they can't accept it. They don't realize it's a normal state of being, that as a lover, and a friend, we use this part of ourselves all the time."

Some people claim Coco Chanel was intuitive to the point of being psychic. She could see into the future, spot needs for which there would later be demand, and had a brilliant knack for creating the right product at the right time.

Some ways to awaken your psychic potential include:

- Meditation

- Yoga

- Aromatherapy

- Mindfulness

- Prayer

- Heart-based spiritual practices

- Free-writing/journaling

- Reading oracle or tarot cards—something which Coco did regularly

Your Challenge

How could you awaken or strengthen your psychic potential?

Engage all your senses so you can feel, taste, touch, smell and hear your future

I have always seen what others do not see; and what they did see, I could not

~ Salvador Dali, artist

REINVENT YOUR LIFE

*I invented my life by taking for granted
that everything I did not like would
have an opposite, which I would like*

~ Coco Chanel

I hope that the quote above is a timely reminder that you can transcend the things you dislike and create a life that fills you with joy—no matter what seemingly insurmountable obstacles block your path. Barry Gibb, one of the members of the British group The Bee Gees, once said, "To go forward, you've got to be unsatisfied."

Clarifying your disappointments and intensifying your desires is an important part of gaining insight about what needs to change. An effective way to do this is to draw up a 'hello, goodbye list'.

Take a blank page and divide it into three columns. In the first column, list all the things you want to leave firmly in the past. Head this 'goodbye.' Head the next column, 'hello' and list all the things that you want to manifest. In the third column, list all the benefits that acting on your 'goodbyes' and 'hellos' will give you.

One of my clients Margaret tried this strategy, and it worked fabulously. Feeling in a rut, and lacking any clarity about what she wanted to do with the rest of her life, she came to me for help.

"What am I going to say to Cassandra," she asked herself as she walked up to the office. She needn't have worried—the fact is that most clients have the solutions to their problems already. I just help tease them out.

After staring at the blank page for a period, her 'hellos' sprouted forth like dormant seeds waiting for the right fertilizer.

Margaret's 'hellos' included: "to follow my heart not my head, to use my skills in a more creative way, take up acting, increase my confidence and self-esteem, spend quality time with my partner."

Margaret's 'goodbyes' included, "Goodbye to working for the Government and feeling suffocated in their overly structured, bureaucratic, rule bound ways of working; being stuck in an office environment; negative thoughts, being scared about leaving my job and not taking action towards my dreams."

How do you think acting on these intentions would benefit Margaret's life?

Here are just a few she identified: "Increased joy, lightness, and energy; feeling more expansive and confident; growth; focus, calm; and strength; identifying and achieving a new career path which is more in tune with my creative, innovative self, and which allows me to use my gifts and favorite skills."

Your Challenge

Reinvent your life. Take the negatives and transform them into positive intentions. Create your own 'hello goodbye list', including the benefits you will feel when you've make the changes

Choose always the way that seems the best, however rough it may be. Custom will soon render it easy and agreeable

~ Pythagoras, mathematician

BOOST YOUR MOTIVATION

A girl should be two things: classy and fabulous

~ Coco Chanel

Being motivated predicts career success better than intelligence, ability, or salary—and there's plenty of research to prove it. Dan Ariely is a professor of behavioral economics at Duke University and the New York Times bestselling author of *Predictably Irrational*. His latest book is *Payoff: The Hidden Logic That Shapes Our Motivations*.

To boost your motivation Ariely suggests:

1. Focus on The Meaning in What You Do

"The things that give us deep happiness are inherently things that take longer and have a big element of meaning in them," he says.

Dan Pink, author of the bestseller, *Drive: The Surprising Truth About What Motivates Us*, says these meaningful things give us purpose. And research shows purpose is one of the most powerful motivators there is.

Purpose, he says is, "Am I doing something in service of a cause larger than myself, or, at the very least, am I making a contribution in my own world?"

2. Take Ownership

If the task you have to do doesn't seem meaningful Pink suggests reframing your experience. "You might not be able to change what you have to do but you can change how you see it. And when you look at it through the lens of how it can help others, you'll often find more motivation."

Gabrielle Chanel was fiercely motivated to make something of her life. She used to toil for hours in the orphanage. She wouldn't allow herself to complain or become disillusioned that this was her lot. That frail, young girl would fiercely scowl at anybody who thought her destiny stopped there.

Her mindset wasn't "I'm slaving away, working for free, wasting my life." In her mind, she wasn't forced to darn and sew. Her reframe was, "I'm learning new skills and sending love into the world." And she never lacked for motivation.

When you feel connected to what you're doing, when you make something your own, you're naturally going to be much more motivated. Autonomy fuels your motivation, as it did Coco's, because, rather than feel you're a slave, you're self-directed. You've claimed some sovereignty over what you do, when you do it, how you do it.

3. Feel "The Intrinsic View"

Often, boosting motivation is just a matter of what part of the activity you focus on before you start a task—getting started, or finishing.

For example, scientific studies show that exercise is one of the most beneficial activities to boost feelings of happiness. Everyone knows this, yet so many of us avoid it. Why? Studies show that it's because we focus on the *beginning* of the workout—which is often the most unpleasant part.

If you think about the middle of the workout when you're feeling in the zone, you receive the advantage of the intrinsic view—you're half way there and you're feeling the benefits. The chances are that by now you're feeling more motivated to keep going.

Take this further by reminding yourself of the intrinsic joy and positive emotions you experience while completing tasks.

Fast-track the intrinsic feeling when your motivation levels are low. Visualize or project yourself to the amazing feelings of accomplishment you'll experience when you've finished. Chant or affirm your feelings of success, "I love finishing! Finishing makes me feel fabulous."

Your Challenge

How can you reframe any doubts, or fears, or disillusionment about your current situation to keep your motivation levels high?

How can you boost motivation and overcome procrastination by feeling "the intrinsic view?" How does finally finishing feel?

Great things are not done by impulse but by a series of small things brought together

~ Vincent van Gogh, artist

MASTER THE ELEMENTAL ART OF SIMPLICITY

Elegance is refusal

~ Coco Chanel

The convent abbey known as Aubazine where Chanel grew up was founded in the 12th century by the saint Étienne d'Obazine. The saintly Étienne had a keen sense of its aesthetics during a period when Western cultural ideas about beauty and proportion were in radical transition.

He and the monks who followed him to this wilderness in a remote corner of south western France were members of a new and rapidly growing Cistercian clerical order, which prized nothing so much as a life and an art of elemental simplicity.

These were formative years—shaping and crafting what would later become Coco Chanel's point of difference—austere grandeur. With her pared back designs, reverence for the simplicity and purity of the colors black and white, and exclusive focus on all things fashion, she proved less really could be more.

We live in an increasingly complicated and cluttered world. If overwhelm or chaos is getting the better of you it may be time to revisit simpler times. Say no to clutter, no to overload—no to anything that smothers the virtuosity of simplicity.

Your Challenge

How can you simplify your life?

What does austere grandeur look like to you?

How will you feel when you have gained freedom from complexity?

Consider working with a clutter coach. One of my clients has started a business doing just that—visit Cate here, http://www.yourcluttercoach.co

Boil it down to what counts the most. What is the essence of what you are trying to do? What is the most important thing? Things only get complicated when you are trying to address too many issues

~ Audrey Hepburn, actress

MAKE A PASSION ACTION PLAN

*Don't spend time beating on a wall,
hoping to transform it into a door*

~ Coco Chanel

Some people think that fate will take care of their future. The winners in life know that failing to plan is planning to fail to make your dreams come true. Success in life is a mixture of good luck and skillful planning. Written goals, with action points and time frames are essential if you really want to achieve a more passionate life.

Of course, not everyone agrees. As you read earlier, some transformational change experts advocate letting things unfold.

It's a balancing act. Only you will know what helps you and what holds you back. Very often the task at hand will determine just how detached you can be.

It's hard to imagine Coco preparing for a collection without a finely executed plan of delivery. So, if you are a 'go with the flow' type and aren't getting the results you desire, quit beating on the 'no planning wall' and take a different path to your success.

Your Challenge

Fuel your burning desire—make a passion action plan. Create a definite outline for carrying out your desire, and begin at once, whether you are ready or not, to put it into motion

Write out a clear, concise statement of your desired outcome. Read your written statement out loud, twice daily—once just before retiring at night, and once after rising in the morning. As you read it, see, feel and believe yourself already in possession of your desire

Do something every day to help move you closer to your goal of leading a more passionate life. To reinforce feelings of success don't forget to tick off and celebrate your achievements along the way

You may say that it is impossible for you to 'see yourself in possession of money' before you actually have it. Here is where a burning desire will come to your aid. If you truly desire money so keenly that your desire is an obsession, you will have no difficulty in convincing yourself that you will acquire it.

The objective is to want money, and to become so determined to have it that you convince yourself you will have it

~ Napoleon Hill, author

AFFIRM THAT YOU DESERVE SUCCESS

I don't do fashion, I AM fashion

~ Coco Chanel

Mary Kay Ash, the founder Mary Kay Cosmetics, preached and practiced that the first step in achieving success is to firmly believe that you are an excellent person who deserves success. In Napoleon Hills's influential bestseller of all time, *Think and Grow Rich*, he shares some of Mary Kay's suggestions:

Imagine yourself successful. Always picture yourself succeeding no matter how dire everything may seem. Visualize the person you desire to become. Set aside time each day to be alone and undisturbed. Get comfortable and relaxed. Close your eyes and concentrate on your desires and goals. See yourself in this new environment—capable and self-confident.

Reflect on your past successes. Every success, be it large or small, is proof that you are capable of achieving more. Record your achievements and refer to them when you begin to lose faith in yourself.

Set definite goals. Have a clear direction of where you want to go. Be aware when you begin to deviate from these goals and take immediate corrective action.

Respond positively to life. Your image, your reactions to life and your decisions are completely within your control. Maintain a positive self-image.

Your Challenge

What three things, if you changed them, would make a positive difference to your self-image, reactions to life and the impact of your decisions?

*Our only limitations are those
we set up in our own minds*

~ Napoleon Hill, author

PRINCIPLE FOUR:

EMPOWER YOUR SPIRIT

SELF-RELIANCE

A woman needs independence from men, not equality. In most cases equality is a step down

~ Coco Chanel

Coco learned from an early age that when all else fails, including the people that are meant to love and support you, you can always rely on yourself.

A singularly independent woman, Coco was a trailblazer during a time when women were still largely dependent on their husbands.

However, in the early years of establishing her career she relied heavily on the good favor of wealthy men and saw purpose in being a kept woman—until such time as she was able to maintain her independence. It was all part of her financial and personal freedom strategy.

Your Challenge

How can you develop more self-reliance?

When you do spend time with others, choose carefully. Don't dilute your energy. Too much group think can stifle your confidence, motivation and originality

Being solitary is not the same as being a loner. Learn from others but cultivate a good relationship with yourself

Keep your own counsel

If you are alone, you belong entirely to yourself. If you are accompanied by even one companion you belong only half to yourself, or even less in proportion to the thoughtlessness of his conduct

~ Leonardo da Vinci, polymath

BELONG TO YOURSELF

*As soon as you set foot on a yacht
you belong to some man, not to
yourself, and you die of boredom*

~ Coco Chanel

Coco Chanel was fiercely independent. This may be in part due to the wounds inflicted in her early childhood by a father who reluctantly married her pregnant mother after Coco's birth, and later abandoned his family.

Some people fear success because they're afraid succeeding might mean having to choose work over intimate relationships. Others fear abandonment.

One of my clients only found her true groove in life when she left an unhealthy marriage—saving her career and her health in the process. Others have found their success is strengthened by the love and support of their significant other.

Only you can determine what your priorities are, how to balance competing demands on your time and energy and what you may, or may not, have to sacrifice. What matters most is maintaining a healthy self-esteem.

Healthy self-esteem means that you don't have to be in a relationship to feel love. You will always have the love you feel for yourself and (ideally) the love you feel for your work. You'll also attract love to you—the love and admiration of people who love you for you and the contribution you make.

Your Challenge

What beliefs do you have about success and relationships? How can you challenge these beliefs safely?

Who do you admire that works and lives with healthy self-love, regardless of others' value judgements?

Understand that the right to choose your own path is a sacred privilege. Use it. Dwell in possibility

~ Oprah Winfrey, businesswoman

GET CREATIVE

*When I can no longer create
anything, I'll be done for*

~ Coco Chanel

"Choose a job that allows the opportunity for some creativity and for spending time with your family. Even if it means less pay—it is better to choose work that is less demanding, that gives you greater freedom, more time to be with your family and friends, engage in cultural activities or just play. I think that is best," His Holiness, The Dalai Lama wrote in his book *The Art of Happiness at Work.*

Not only do creative people get to do cool stuff, but they use their brains in the biggest way possible. They listen to and use both sides of their brains for maximum impact.

A few years ago, there was an article about the most desired recruits for medical school. Guess who they were? Students who were majoring in music. The reason was reported to be that their left and right brains are equally developed because music is mathematical and creative at the same time.

The same point could be made for people who blend creativity with business—both draw on differing, but complementary, sides of the brain.

Creativity is also related to intuition—a powerful, non-rational and innovative and decision making tool. More and more people and businesses are tapping into the power of intuition to help them achieve phenomenal results.

Powerful creativity is highly spiritual too. When you create you bring your whole soul into being and you enter a transcendental, meditative state —something psychologist Mihaly Csikszentmihaly refers to as 'flow.'

He and other success experts maintain that natural abundance flows from getting into this state and involving yourself in things that increase positive feelings like inner excitement. I call this passion. Others call it love or joy.

Daniel Pink the author of A *Whole New Mind said,* "The future belongs to a very different kind of person with a very different kind of mind—creators and empathizers, pattern recognizers and meaning makers. These people, he predicts, will now reap society's richest rewards and share its greatest joys."

Here's just a few things creativity can do for you:

- Increase your spiritual connection

- Enable you to access elevated levels of consciousness, higher imagination, intuition, the artistic level of the unconscious which is where the artist's magic lies

- Tap into your authenticity and true essence

- Relax your over-worked analytical mind

- Re-energize your flagging spirits

- Provide a wonderful escape from the 'real' world

- Encourage whole-brain learning

- Boost your intelligence and increase your likelihood of success

Your Challenge

When are the times you feel a sense of inner joy or flow?

How can you make more time for creativity?

How can you solve a problem or challenge innovatively?

Art washes from the soul the dust of everyday life

~ Pablo Picasso, artist

CHANGE YOUR NAME

My father was not there

~ Coco Chanel

A radical change in name is one's commitment to a higher personal calling and is not uncommon among creative people, writes Twyla Tharp in *The Creative Habit: Learn It and Use It for Life.*

Used well, a change of name can be globally memorable and a fulfilling prophecy of future success. Numerous successful people have achieved outstanding fame writing under a pen name or pseudonym. Mozart played with multiple variations of his birth name most of his life, as did Marilyn Monroe and Coco Chanel.

Coco Chanel's real name is as enigmatic as the lady herself—shrouded in mystery and cloaked in a layer of her own story-telling. One of the enduring mysteries surrounding her is exactly how she got her nickname. Some of her biographers accept the story that her father called her "Coco."

Others contend that she came by the name during her brief stint as a cabaret singer because her repertoire consisted of only two songs: "Ko ko ri Ko" and " Quiqu`a vu Coco?" But according to one source, Coco once explained that the name was nothing more than a shortened version of "coquette," the French word for "kept woman."

Coco rarely talked about the circumstances of her birth, but once said that she was named in part after one of the nuns in the hospital poorhouse for illegitimate children where she was born.

Her name was Gabrielle Bonheur, according to Coco. However, the name Bonheur does not appear on her baptismal certificate. Bonheur in French means "happiness" and Coco may have created this story to lay claim to its meaning.

She was a child of the poorhouse, plain Gabrielle Chasnel (a version of her surname which also exists in historical records, and which she claims was an error). She remained Gabrielle for most of her childhood—the nickname "Coco" which she adopted, and for which she became famous, is also anchored in untruths regarding its origin. In some versions, she says her father called her "Little Coco." because he never liked "Gabrielle."

It is said that she thought, 'Coco' was an awful name yet she was proud of its recognition throughout the world. The infamous courtesan Mata Hari, was proud of her fame too. Her real name was Margaretha Zelle— later she was forced to adopt her married name MacLeod, before ditching them both to pursue independence (and infamy) as a dancer and courtesan in Paris.

Both women shared a tragic past from which they sought permanent escape, and both sought independence through fame. And both yearned to be loved.

Interestingly the name on Coco's tombstone she designed for herself simply says, 'Gabrielle Chanel.' It has a simple cross, and five lions heads.

Your Challenge

How could you experiment with a new name and new identity?

How could 'hiding' behind a false name give you confidence and courage?

You're not a star until they can spell your name in Karachi

~ Humphrey Bogart, actor

PRAY

*J'aime la vie! I feel that to
live is a wonderful thing*

~ Coco Chanel

As Justine Picardie writes in her excellent book, *The Secret Life of Coco Chanel*, Coco never admitted to her years at Aubazine, where she lived from the age of 11 to 18, in an orphanage run by the sisters of the Congregation of the Sacred Heart of Mary.

But the fact was that Coco spent much of her early years there. The ritual of prayer was a constant part of daily life, and foreseeably a source of nourishment— filling her with hope that, despite being abandoned by her father, and knowing she was penniless, her life would be beautiful.

"Prayer is when you talk to God; Meditation is when you listen to God," says author Diana Robinson. Others refer to the voice of God as tapping in to their intuition, higher self, inner goddess or Sacred Divine. Whatever your belief system, prayer is a form of spiritual communion.

Many people have lost their union with God because of the hypocritical dogma which has polluted many faith systems. As author Paulo Coelho, shares on the back jacket of his book, *The Spy*—a fascinating story about Mata Hari, 'He has experimented with magic and alchemy, studied philosophy and religion, read voraciously, lost and recovered his faith, and experienced the pain and pleasure of love.

'In searching for his own place in the world, he has discovered answers for the challenges that everybody faces. He believes that within ourselves, we have the necessary strength to find our destiny.'

One of the key tools that have given him strength is prayer. As he writes in the foreword to his book, "O Mary, conceived without sin, pray for us who have recourse to You. Amen."

'Scientific (4-step) prayer therapy is the only really answer to the great deception,' writes Joseph Murphy (PhD.) in his excellent book, *The Miracle of Mind Dynamics*. 'Let the light of God shine in your mind, and you will neutralize the harmful effects of the negatives implanted in your subconscious mind.'

The four steps include:

1. Recognition of the healing presence of Infinite intelligence

2. Complete acceptance of the One Power

3. Affirmation of the Truth

4. Rejoice and give thanks for the answer

The indicator of God's presence in you is the presence of peace, harmony, abundance, and perfect health.

Your Challenge

Embark on scientific prayer therapy

Take the time to stop and pray from your heart. The words that you use aren't as important compared to the strength of your desire to connect with The Divine

Be open to a response appearing which is different from your expectations—and know that your prayers are heard and answered

Faith in action is love

~ Mother Theresa

MAINTAIN YOUR FAITH

I've done my best, in regard to people and to life, without precepts, but with a taste for justice

~ Coco Chanel

Very often the results you want to achieve take time to appear. Without faith, doubts and disbelief can sabotage your chances of success. Getting discouraged, feeling pessimistic, or giving up are some of the common reasons people fail. Mother Theresa once said, 'By transforming faith into living acts of love, we put ourselves in contact with God.'

Coco Chanel was a woman of faith. She knew the power of cultivating and maintaining unwavering belief. Her faith was always driven by love. Love of the clothes she designed, love of the perfume she created, love of the people's lives she transformed—whether through her patronage or the things she made. And her faith was also driven by her passion for justice.

Faith is not always about spirituality or religion—faith can be about your belief in your ability to succeed. It's as much about your dedication to not be something, but to be someone—your glorious, successful self!

Julia Cameron, an active artist and author of *The Artist's Way,* and another thirty or so fiction, and non-fiction books, advocates relinquishing too much effort. She suggests turning energy instead from stressful striving, to cultivating faith and trust.

Prayer, gratitude, acceptance and unwavering belief that everything happens for a reason are just some of the many strategies she encourages people to embrace.

Your Challenge

How can you maintain your faith?

Tap into the awesome power of meditation, yoga and a spiritual faith-based perspective to help you maintain a positive expectancy, manage stress and increase your intuitive, creative powers

Empower your faith in your vision—visualize your goal as already achieved

Empower your faith in yourself—create some positive affirmations and say them regularly

Be of service—transform your faith into living acts of love

Identify some ways you can take action—even when you feel the odds are stacked against you, or you feel like giving up

If faith is something you'd like to cultivate, you'll find encouragement throughout my *Mid-Life Career Rescue* series. You may also like to check out Julia's book *Faith and Will*, or find your own sources of sustenance.

To pray is to let go and let God take over

~ Philippians 4:6-7

CONSULT THE ORACLES

*I don't care what you think about me.
I don't think about you at all*

~ Coco Chanel

Tarot and other subjects such as astrology, alternative healing, psychic phenomena, spirituality, and a fascination with the Goddess legends captured Coco Chanel's interest. She, like many people, found great wisdom, peace, comfort and healing from an eclectic array of spiritual rituals.

As the astrologer, Jessica Adams, shares on her website, "Coco Chanel used the Lenormand oracle card deck to help her in business—as well as in her personal life. As my friend, Justine Picardie explains in her acclaimed biography of Chanel, 'the cards still rest where she left them, lying in a moment frozen in time, in her apartment in Paris.'"

Coco was taught the precepts of theosophy by the first and foremost love of her life, the English playboy, Captain Arthur Edward "Boy" Capel (CBE).

Theosophy is defined by some sources as, "A collection of mystical and occultist philosophies concerning, or seeking direct knowledge of, the presumed mysteries of life and nature, particularly of the nature of divinity and the origin and purpose of the universe."

My first experience with psychic phenomena and the tarot was when I was a teenager in New Zealand in the late 70s. A friend had given her baby up for adoption and asked me to come with her to visit a psychic for a reading.

I remember feeling both apprehensive and excited. I was amazed that the reading revealed such true things about my life, and I knew then that there was something special about tarot cards.

Like Coco, it's a fascination that stayed with me throughout my life and which continues to provide inspiration courage and fortitude—both personally and professionally. No one knows exactly how tarot cards originated. The earliest tarot deck dates back to the 1400s Renaissance Italy.

'I've come to believe that a lot of wisdom was incorporated in the tarot. I feel, as others do, that the ancient keepers of the old ways or earth-based spirituality, wanted to pass on information,' writes Karen Vogel in the introduction to her *Motherpeace Tarot Guidebook.*

'As warfare increasingly became a way of life in the Dark Ages of Europe, old ways were lost as whole cities and civilizations were wiped out.

'It was more and more difficult to pass on oral and written traditions since whole cultures were destroyed and ancient libraries burned. One of the traditional stories about the origins of the tarot is that the wisdom keepers in these cultures were the storytellers, artists and healers.

They chose between writing a spiritual or philosophical text or putting the knowledge into a game. They decided that a game in the form of cards would last longer, be more accessible to everyone, and easier to hide.'

By the time of the Renaissance, Christianity had dominated Europe as both a political and religious powerhouse. Millions of women, who were often the healers and spiritual leaders, were murdered during the Inquisition.

Those who threatened Church authority or knew about ritual and healing, either died or went into hiding, taking certain information with them. It was in this atmosphere that tarot began and subsequently spread all over Europe.

Of all the psychological theories in the West, that of revered Swiss psychologist Carl Jung stands out as most applicable to Tarot.

Jung wrote about Tarot on several occasions, seeing it as depicting archetypes of transformation like those he found in myths, dreams and alchemy.

He described its divinatory abilities as similar to the IChing and astrology, and late in life established a group who attempted to integrate insights about a person based on multiple divination systems including Tarot.

Jessica Adams also notes, "This connection with astrology is not something that the house of Chanel shies away from today. In fact, I vividly remember Karl Lagerfeld's illustration of the zodiac sign Sagittarius, decorating my horoscope column in Vogue Australia."

Astrology also played a major role in Lagerfeld's campaign for the perfume Chance, where a lion play a key role. The 'Chanel-Leo' is very important when understanding the house of Chanel, the woman who created it—and the fragrance.

Jessica Adams also suggests that one of the cards in Coco's Lenormand deck inspired one of the secret ingredients contained in Chanel N°5, ". . . this card shows a beautiful green tree, seven love hearts and the message . . . 'A tree far away means good health—when near—illness there will be, many trees close together means things will turn out all right, you'll see.'

As we now know, a naturally occurring tree moss is one of the secret ingredients in Chanel N°5 fragrance. A coincidence? Or did Chanel bring together astrology and the Lenormand when choosing her blend?"

Your Challenge

Experiment with tarot—either have a reading with an experienced tarot card reader, or study the cards and their meanings for yourself

Feed your curiosity—take note of the places and circumstances where tarot, astrological symbols and other mystical and occultist philosophies are used—in business and life

How could you blend astrology and tarot into your career and life?

*He who has a mind to understand,
let him understand*

~ Mary Magdalene, in The Gospel of Mary

PRINCIPLE FIVE:

EMPOWER YOUR MIND

FAITH IN YOUR STARS

Arrogance is in everything I do. It is in my gestures, the harshness of my voice, in the glow of my gaze, in my sinewy, tormented face

~ Coco Chanel

Much of Coco Chanel's success can be attributed to her faith in the stars. Chanel believed in astrology. She was a Leo, symbolized by the lion, queen of the beasts. Leo is the sign of royalty. Proud and arrogant, yet loyal and brave, this sign is ablaze with warmth and fire.

Creative entrepreneurship is the true stamp of a Leo—and Chanel manifested this in buckets—driven by passion, purpose, determination, a desire to lead not follow, the courage and fearlessness of a lion, and a serious need to be noticed.

Making an impression is Priority One for many Leos—think Mick Jagger, Arnold Schwarzenegger, Jennifer Lopez, and other flamboyant people who share Coco Chanel's sun.

Chanel's moon was in Pisces, making her intuitive to the point of being psychic, writes Karen Karbo in *The Gospel According to Coco Chanel*. This may explain her uncanny knack for predicting where best to place her energy to amass a great following and fortune.

Leo is also the fifth sign of the zodiac—a number Coco used to astounding success when she named her perfume, Chanel N°5. She also leveraged off her faith in her stars and other spiritual tools to empower her mind, and sustain her during periods of darkness.

"Most clients come with financial problems or relationship problems," my friend and astrologer Marianne O'Hagan says. "They come looking for the hope of happiness in the future."

Marianne knows me personally and professionally. You can read more of her story in *Mid-Life Career Rescue: What Makes You Happy*—including how she started her own business by using her faith in the stars.

I'm a Libra in Western astrology and a Snake in Chinese astrology. It's true when they say that Libran's love harmony, balance and beauty. I love it when I receive feedback from readers, saying my book is "beautifully written."

Or, as a person who read the first book in The *Art of Success* series, inspired by Leonardo da Vinci, posted in their review, *"This beautiful book wraps art around business and life and makes each hum with energy and creativity and brings the reader new vitality."*

Google 'best careers' for Snakes and I'm told to avoid careers where I have to work too hard. 'Working hard' to me is doing something I dislike, working with people who don't care. Working hard for me also involves not marching to my own beat.

But when I'm working in the passion zone, fulfilling my purpose, and living my values, now that's a different story.

Whether you're a believer in the notion that whatever planets align at your time and place of birth can determine your intrinsic strengths, shape your character, relationships and fortunes, there's plenty of helpful data to aid you in your quest for success. Keep an open mind and don't take everything as true.

Your Challenge

Go cosmic—gain additional insight about your astrological sign from any of the plethora of books, online resources and personal astrologers

Focus on identifying your strengths, Achilles heel, and best-fit-factors career-wise and in your personal life

I liked the idea that astrology believes we all are special and have unique gifts. It was at that moment that my love of astrology was born

~ Marianne O'Hagan, astrologer

BOOST YOUR SELF-AWARENESS

I'm neither smart nor stupid, but I don't think I'm a run-of-the-mill person. I've been in business without being a businesswoman, I've loved without being a woman made only for love

~ Coco Chanel

How can you be true to yourself if you don't know who you are and who you want to be?

Astrology is just one of many helpful tools to boost self-awareness. But very often it provides just a small part of the puzzle of discovering your authentic self.

Leonardo da Vinci once said, "The acquisition of knowledge is always of use to the intellect, because it may thus drive out useless things and retain the good."

While Leonardo clearly didn't have access to modern personality tests he was a master in the realms of observation. He knew what gave him energy, how he preferred to take in information, make decisions and organize his life.

The Myers Briggs Type Indicator is one of the most popular preference-based personality assessment tools.

Experts differ as to whether Leonardo's personality preferences were INTP (Introverted, Intuitive, Thinking, and Perceiving), or ISTP (Introverted, Sensing, Thinking, and Perceiving), or even an ENTP (Extroverted, Intuitive, Thinking, and Perceiving).

While guesswork is rarely accurate some people believe that Coco Chanel shared a similar personality to Leonardo—the main difference lay in her ability to plan, schedule and start and finish the projects she committed to—making her possibly an INTJ.

For more information about The Myers Briggs Type Indicator, turn to Google or consult a registered MBTI practitioner for an accurate assessment.

Neuropsychologist, Katherine Benziger says, "People are happiest, healthiest and most effective when developing, using and being rewarded for their natural gifts." This is very true.

Paying greater attention to the things that stir your soul, ignite your passion, and awaken your heart are also great ways to boost your self-awareness.

Your Challenge

Who are you? What are your natural gifts? What are your super-powers?

How can you do and be what you are?

Make boosting your awareness of your true essence your priority

Keep a passion journal, and notice all the times, people and events that make your spirit soar

What comes naturally to you? Who are you, and what can you do, without really *trying*?

Notice the times you feel marvelous

The more you know about yourself the better your decisions will be. You'll also have better success in presenting yourself and your natural talents in the best light—to others and yourself.

Do you know what you are? You are a marvel. You are unique. In all the years that have passed, there has never been another child like you. Your legs, your arms, your clever fingers, the way you move. You may become a Shakespeare, a Michelangelo, a Beethoven. You have the capacity for anything. Yes, you are a marvel

~ Pablo Casal, musician

CREATE A NEW LIFE STORY

A girl should be two things:
who and what she wants

~ Coco Chanel

No one will ever know the real Coco Chanel, because she designed it that way. She once said, "People's lives are an enigma."

She perpetrated her own mystery by constantly creating a new life story, reinventing her past and weaving around and around her family history.

It wasn't a history she was proud of. She felt the stigma of her illegitimate birth in a poorhouse to parents who, for all intents and purposes, were wandering gypsies.

To live the fantasy that sustained her as a young girl locked in a convent, she imagined a new life—and with it a new life story about her background.

She obscured her past from others, refashioning its heartaches and betrayals, smoothing away the rough edges. She reengineered her history just as she recut the sleeves of a dress, unfastening seams that pinched, cutting unsightly threads, and then sewing it back together.

Coco once said, "I don't like the family. You're born in it, not of it. I don't know anything more terrifying than the family . . . Childhood—you speak of it when you're very tired, because it's a time when you had hopes, and expectations."

Like real stories in books and movies, your life story will have a hero (you), a quest, obstacles to overcome to achieve the story goal and a climax—and hopefully, a happy ending.

Your Challenge

Who are you? What's your story? We live the lives we imagine. Retell your story—leaving out the bits you don't want to relive

If your childhood didn't meet your expectations, if your family or personal history feels like a hindrance, or if you are dragging around the baggage of a disappointing, hurtful or traumatic past—*act as if* you had a different past.

Create a new historical account of the life you lived—as long as your intention is not to create fraud and ruin lives

How can we rewrite our life story so that pain becomes meaningful and actually promotes growth and transformation?

~ Catherine Ann Jones, author of *Heal Your Self with Writing*

ACCENT THE POSITIVE

There have been several Duchesses of Westminster but there is only one Chanel!

~ Coco Chanel

Coco and the Duke of Westminster enjoyed a decade-long love affair. Destined to be a lover and never a wife, she was said to have been devastated when the man she regarded as her greatest love, Boy Capel, married Lady Diana Wyndhaman, an English aristocrat. Capel was never faithful to her, or to anyone, and the affair continued after his marriage.

Coco always accented the positive—no matter how bitterly her heart was crushed. Whether it was ego, pride or with a practical realization that giving in to forlorn thoughts would never be a winning formula, Coco modeled positivity.

When you let desire not fear propel you forward, magic happens. It's the Law of Attraction; The Law of Manifestation; The Law of Intention. But it only works if you stay positive. Negativity is a repellent. Positivity is a magnet, drawing abundance forward.

Your Challenge

How can you stay positive even when things look bleak?

Set your horizons high, believe in the beauty of your dreams and don't settle for less

Negative thoughts are like weeds—they grow untended, positive thoughts are like flowers—you need to nurture them every day

~ His Holiness, The Dalai Lama

FAILURE IS NOT FATAL

Success is most often achieved by those who don't know that failure is inevitable

~ Coco Chanel

Oprah Winfrey once said, "I have a lot of things to prove to myself. One is that I can live my life fearlessly."

It's a sentiment Mademoiselle Chanel took to heart with the courage and fierce determination of Leo the Lion.

Although Coco is widely recognized as one of the world's greatest fashionistas, she also made colossal mistakes and suffered staggering failures which would have felled many.

But she persevered anyway. She knew that learning from her own experiences also meant learning from her mistakes.

"The French fashion press lay in wait for her first post-war collection," Justine Picardie writes in, *Coco Chanel: The Legend and The Life,* "like cats at a rat hole."

Her desire to relaunch her career in America was a massive public failure. She had worked tirelessly on the collection, despite being ill with a stoppage in her intestine.

So, the damning reviews condemning her efforts as 'a sad retrospective,' and 'a failure to engage with fashion,' were even more cruel. Other critics attacked her personally.

A woman less sure of herself would have been humiliated and quit. But their attack only served to stir her fighting blood.

She didn't put away her scissors nor her inventor's hat. She never lost the courage to continue—driven by a determination for justice and to prove her critics wrong.

She learned from her failures, accepted them as par for the course, and continued her pioneering quest to learn, experiment, explore—and triumph.

Your Challenge

What new experiences are you prepared to embark on? Are you prepared to fail in order to succeed?

What would you do differently if you had no fear of failing spectacularly?

Whose failure story inspires you? Why? What does it teach you?

Reframe failure. The greatest lessons come not from your successes but from your failures. What can you allow your failures to teach you? Don't look at hurdles as a negative thing but as a reflective tool on how to improve.

Reading biographies of people like Coco Chanel, Leonardo da Vinci and other people whose success you admire can give you great encouragement along the path to creating your own victories.

Success is not final, failure is not fatal: it is the courage to continue that counts

~ Winston Churchill, politician

MAKE MISTAKES

I am continuing, I shall continue.
They'll end up understanding

~ Coco Chanel

So many people stagnate under the weight of perfectionism because they worry about making mistakes.

It may be challenging, but investing in strategies to create more tolerance and acceptance towards making mistakes will prove liberating.

Sometimes the greatest fortune comes from making the biggest blunders. Here's just a few mistakes that turned out well:

- The renowned Stradivarius violin became the world's finest and most costly musical instrument by mistake

- The modern pacemaker was born from an error by its developer who inadvertently put the wrong sized resistor into his nascent heart rhythm device

- Charles Goodyear of tire empire fame, accidentally boiled a brew of rubber and sulfur.

When he returned to his chemical stew he found a versatile new plastic

- Inventor, Spencer Silver, had been attempting to develop an ultra-strength adhesive for 3M laboratories, but instead developed a sticky substance that could easily be pulled off. His colleague used the glue to hold his hymnbook bookmark in place and the first post-it was born

- Alexander Fleming left a number of laboratory Petri dishes unwashed and returned to find that many of them had been contaminated and grown bacteria colonies. However, on one he noted that a patch of mold had prevented the growth of bacteria which prompted him to explore the substance's bacteria-killing properties

- Musician Ornette Coleman's mistake led her to be acclaimed as the inventor of 'free jazz.' She was awarded the MacArthur Fellowship (nicknamed the Genius Award) in 1994 and the Pulitzer Prize for Music in 2007

- Coco Chanel's critics said she made a mistake when she attempted to relaunch her fashion house after the war. French and British journalists called her comeback collection, "A flop." But, others, including the influential editor at Harpers Bazaar, Dianne Vreeland, ran front-page spreads. Unexpected support from her business partner Wertheimer, also ended a three-decade long feud. "I am continuing, I shall continue. They'll end up understanding," Coco famously said.

Your Challenge

Buoy your resolve by collecting stories about other people who were treated harshly by peers, critics, family and other disbelievers

Collect a file of inspiring stories about mistakes that turned out well

Refuse to be a victim. Next time you feel you've made a mistake, ask yourself, "How could this work out for my highest good?" or "What can I learn?"

Be gentle with yourself. Sometimes making mistakes heralds a time of new birth and energy. Draw on the lessons you have learned to help you move forward

Notice how you have grown and changed as a result of everything that has happened. Gather information as you go and be ready for a new adventure. Look for positive signs for successful outcomes in the future

It was when I found out I could make mistakes that I knew I was on to something

~ Ornette Coleman, Musician

BOOST YOUR BELIEF

A woman needs independence from men, not equality. In most cases equality is a step down

~ Coco Chanel

It's the messages you tell yourself that matter most, says celebrity hypnotherapist and author, Marisa Peers. "Belief without talent will get you further than talent with no belief. If you have the two you will be unstoppable."

Coco Chanel believed from a very early age that the bridge to her freedom and self-respect lay in securing and maintaining her independence.

She also believed in the power of being loved as a woman. She had no desire to be a man—only to be adored by them. "A woman who is not loved is no woman", she once said.

Many people mistakenly sacrifice their relationships in pursuit of successful careers. Unhelpful beliefs, including, "You can't have it all" or, "You can't have a relationship and be successful," may partly be to blame.

You may not be aware of your own self-limiting beliefs and patterns, or the negative, confining impact of others' beliefs about what you should be doing with your life. Perhaps you've defined your life according to what others think you are capable of, or believe you should settle for.

Even when the answers are clear you may resist the changes needed to achieve more happiness and passion in your work or personal life. Fear often lies at the heart of this reluctance or resistance.

Viktor Frankl, a psychiatrist and survivor of the Nazi concentration camps, believes that the cause of people's fear is a basic and crippling lack of faith about themselves and their capacity to make positive and successful changes.

To get at some of the core beliefs standing between you and the success you desire ask yourself, "I'll do anything to achieve (insert goal/dream) just don't ask me to do that (insert the fear or belief that holds you back).

Acknowledge the things you don't believe and challenge them. Interview your beliefs, by asking them the following questions.

"Where's your evidence for that?" (That being whatever you fear or hold to be true?)

"What's the worst that could happen if you pursued your passion? How bad would that really be? How can you increase the likelihood of success?"

"What tells you that you could follow your dreams?" (A nice shift from focusing on the problem, to looking for solutions instead).

"What have you tried recently that worked? What you are you doing now that works?"

"Who do you know that is happy at work? What could you learn from them?"

"How does your (supportive other) know you can do this? What difference will it make to them when you are happier and more successful?"

You'll find other helpful strategies to challenge self-limiting beliefs in my book, *Boost Your Self-Esteem and Confidence: Six Easy Steps to Increase Self-Confidence, Self-esteem, Self-Value and Love Yourself More.*

I've also included a helpful section in my book, *Mid-Life Career Rescue: What Makes You Happy*. In this book, I share my experience following reading *The Biology of Belief: Unleashing the Power of Consciousness, Matter & Miracles*, by Dr. Bruce Lipton.

Your Challenge

So often we aren't even aware of what our self-limiting beliefs are. If your beliefs are ingrained, or you keep sabotaging your own success, seeking help from a qualified practitioner with expertise in reprogramming stubborn, disempowering beliefs may be a game-changer

Chances are you don't need to see a therapist to move beyond self-limiting beliefs, but if you do, go and get help. There's magic in that

You can also learn from some of the most powerful, effective and simple techniques used by practitioners working in the realm of positive psychology and mind reprogramming—including hypnosis

I told my audience that if they changed their beliefs they could change their lives

~ Dr. Bruce Lipton, cell biologist

PRINCIPLE SIX:

EMPOWER YOUR BODY

SHARPEN YOUR MOST POTENT TOOL WITH SCENT

Fashion is not something that exists in dresses only. Fashion is in the sky, in the street, fashion has to do with ideas, the way we live, what is happening

~ Coco Chanel

Along with your skills and capabilities, it is your state of mind that determines how successful and happy you will be. There are many ways to empower your mind—working with essential oils is one of the most effortless.

Coco knew the alchemical potency of flowers and plants. She surrounded herself with nature's elixir and amassed a fortune from the essential oils which helped make her perfume Chanel N°5 famous.

Here's a few other essential oils and natural therapeutic remedies to lend your mind a helping hand:

1. Laurel Essential Oil: Motivates people who lack energy or confidence. Strengthens the memory and helps maintain concentration, especially during prolonged tasks

2. Rosemary Essential Oil: Instills confidence during periods of self-doubt and keeps motivation

levels high when the going gets tough. It is also said to help maintain an open mind and to make you more welcoming of new ideas.

3. Cardamom Essential Oil Stimulates a dull mind, dispels tensions and worries, and nurtures and supports the brain and nervous system. Many people find it of great support during challenging times.

4. Peppermint Essential Oil: With its refreshing scent peppermint works like a power boost for your fatigued mind, making you feel sharper and more alert.

Your Challenge

Read more about aromatherapy for achievers and learn about essential oils for success

Sharpen your most potent tools—your heart and your mind. Become a perfumer—experiment with essential oils until you find a winning blend

If you believe in aromatherapy . . . it works! If you don't believe in aromatherapy . . . it works!

~ Cristina Proano-Carrion, aromatherapist

RESTORE YOUR ENERGY

Those who create are rare; those who cannot are numerous. Therefore, the latter are stronger

~ Coco Chanel

Coco loved her work, but she still made time to rest. Your physical and emotional health is better supported by investing in gentle rituals that restore and energize you.

Yet in today's world being busy is often worn like a "badge of honor," says author and nutritional biochemist, Dr. Libby.

"Many people see rest as failure," she says. "However regularly finding space so that you can rest is one of the best health investments you can make.

If you are seeking permission to rest, or simply looking for some restorative strategies here are a few ideas to help you:

1. Wake 30 minutes earlier than your household. While not technically resting, creating space for some morning rituals can create an unparalleled sense of calm. Rising earlier than everyone else will enable you to make the most of the peacefulness that morning can

bring. Find a quiet spot and set your intentions for the day.

2. You may also enjoy the art of writing morning pages. Julia Cameron, in her most excellent book *The Artist's Way* (a must read), recommends writing morning pages every day. The writing is just stream of consciousness, writing out whatever you are feeling—good (or what one of my clients calls the "sunnies") or not so good ("the uglies")

It's a way of clearing the mind, "a farewell to what has been and a hello to what will be," Julia says. "Write down just what is crossing your consciousness. Cloud thoughts that move across consciousness. Meeting your shadow and taking it out for a cup of coffee so it doesn't eddy your consciousness during the day."

3. Pablo Picasso once said, "Art washes from the soul the dust of everyday life." Creating art can be a wonderfully meditative, tranquil practice. Your work of art doesn't have to be brilliant, and you don't have to share it with the world. It doesn't even need to involve paint or canvas. It may be as simple as coloring in.

4. Float. Artist, Mark Olson, cares for his body and soul by spending time in his personal flotation chamber (a light-and sound-proof tank filled with water).

An added benefit of this gentle practice is that it provides him with further inspiration. You may not have access to a flotation chamber, but just soaking in some water can be hugely therapeutic.

5. Meditate. "It's a little like exercise," says British actor, Jude Law. "It stops me overthinking and focuses my actions. What won me around was that I was in my early 40s and wasn't able to find 20 or 30 minutes a day just to sit and think.

"It seems appalling that out of the long day that's something we find so hard to do and suddenly it became a necessity to leave all the stuff, not answer anything, just breathe and try to be."

6. Improve your sleep. Many of us have little or no transition into rest, says Dr. Libby. "We simply put a head on the pillow and expect to switch off. A simple meditation focusing on your breath is a way to ease into rest.

"Lay on the floor, or on the bed, or sit supported in a chair, whatever you prefer. Bring your focus to your breath moving in and out of your nostrils."

If you need additional help there are many wonderful guided meditation videos and audio is available online. Use these as a guide to help you find what works for you.

7. Coco was a prolific reader and surrounded herself with books. There is often nothing more replenishing than a good read. Introverted time spent by yourself can be incredibly restorative.

New research also suggests that reading books every day can help you live longer. A study published by US researchers in the academic journal, Social Science & Medicine, concluded that, "Book reading provides a survival advantage amongst the elderly."

Your Challenge

What restores and energizes you?

How much do you read? Pick up a physical book and take a break from your screen

Create a restorative morning ritual

Invest in yourself, as I often do—including regular massages, reflexology, technology detox days, and maintaining boundaries—to protect valuable introverted "me time"

Our brains never get a break and the results can be increased stress, anxiety, insomnia and, if left unchecked, even depression. But there is something you can do—nothing

~ Mathew Johnstone, author and cartoonist

SURROUND YOURSELF WITH NATURE

Nature gives you the face you have at twenty; it is up to you to merit the face you have at fifty

~ Coco Chanel

Coco loved to be surrounded by flowers and to spend time walking amongst, or gazing upon, nature to replenish. "I often found her alone sitting at her dressing table, gazing down into the garden, looking at the chestnut trees," recounts Claude Delay, now an imminent psychoanalyst, who knew Coco in her youth.

We all know the physical benefits of nature—being amongst plants and flowers boosts mental well-being. A series of published studies has shown clear links between gardening and positivity.

One study found levels of the stress hormone cortisol in those who gardened were considerably lower those who people who relaxed by reading.

Even the simple act of looking out a window to green space has been linked to reduced stress levels and faster recovery from illness.

"The garden brings stillness," says Lisa, a marketing executive who says she couldn't have survived her working life without a garden.

"Touching the soil is one of the most reenergizing things I can do. Everything slows down. My mind works differently.

"I don't set out to solve problems but the answers seem to come. These days if ever I am stressed it will be because I haven't been in the garden."

Similarly, Lisa—who suffers from anxiety and depression—finds solace in a small vegetable garden she started behind her flat.

"When I become immobilized by my anxiety, the garden gives me something achievable to get started on. Gardening is methodical I can go out there and think, 'What does my garden need?'

"It could be as simple as pulling caterpillars off some broccoli. Tuning in to this helps me get more in touch with things outside of myself."

Your Challenge

Experience the healing power of nature. Whether you're blessed with green fingers or not, it doesn't matter what you do—just that you get outside and surround yourself with some green space every day

Monitor how much time you spend indoors. Schedule regular fresh air time

Beauty surrounds us,
but usually we need to be walking
in a garden to know it

~ Rumi, Persian poet

WALK!

There is nothing more comfortable than a caterpillar and nothing more made for love than a butterfly. We need dresses that crawl and dresses that fly. Fashion is at once a caterpillar and a butterfly— caterpillar by day, butterfly by night

~ Coco Chanel

Coco Chanel spent much of her youth walking up and down the staircase, with its 36 stairs, leading from the orphanage to the French Abbey of Aubazine—over and over again, from Vespers to Matins for over 7 years.

Did she sprint down the stairs—eager to get back to bed? Or did she walk slowly, her eyes down on the stairs, her head bowed in prayer? Whether going to the Abby felt like a penance or a meditation Coco never said. But the emotional, mental and spiritual benefits for maintaining regular exercise, like walking, is well documented—boosting spirits, rejuvenating mental energy, and energizing the body.

When your breathing is calm and steady you are in a nurtured state, which also helps strengthen your immune system. Researchers also confirm there is a strong link between breathing, outside energy and beneficial brainwave patterns.

This may explain why so many people say that walking is their meditation—clearing their mind, and allowing space for good ideas to flourish.

Your Challenge

Discipline yourself to go for a walk regularly—ideally outside and somewhere not too frenzied

Oxygenate your mind and body—combine brisk walking with deep breathing to boost your energy levels, short-term memory, and state of mind

Walking for me is my way of thinking, my way of meditating. It is not that I am thinking, but that I am in a kind of trance totally connected to the present moment

~ Paulo Coelho, author

HEALTHY SPIRITUAL SIGNIFICANCE

Remember me, on earth or in heaven

~ Coco Chanel

"If we have unhealthy thoughts and feelings about our spiritual significance and life purpose we're more likely to have concerns with the following health problems: heart attack, stroke, cancer, or other life-threatening disease: a major automobile accident, fall or other serious mishap." says Dr. Mona Lisa Schultz, a neuropsychiatrist and medical intuitive.

By rewiring your feelings and thoughts about your life's purpose and spiritual connection, you'll improve the health of your 'seventh' emotional center—imbuing you with a sense of purpose in life, and a connection with the universe and a higher power.

To move toward health in the seventh emotional center involves overcoming a lifelong emotional pattern of hopelessness and despair—something Coco Chanel battled to conquer throughout her life.

Your Challenge

Feel as lovers do—unite with a higher power. Affirm your life purpose and sacred mission in life and feel more joyous

Remind yourself of your life purpose, free yourself from grudges and resentments, and access a higher power

To foster the ability to change in spite of your fears use affirmations. For example, "I know I am worthwhile. It is safe for me to succeed. I love and appreciate myself." Or use some other empowering affirmation to remind yourself that you are powerful, talented and worthy.

Research suggests that affirmations are more powerful when "I" is replaced by "you." For example, "You are powerful, talented and worthy." Curious? Check out the findings here— http://bit.ly/2obPZ47

Compose your life in service to your God—help make the world a better place

I was born out of due time in the sense that by temperament and talent I should have been more suited for the life of a small Bach, living in anonymity and composing regularly for an established service and for God

~ Igor Stravinsky, composer

YOUR BODY BAROMETER

I am not young but I feel young. The day I feel old, I will go to bed and stay there. J'aime la vie! I feel that to live is a wonderful thing

~ Coco Chanel

Feeling tired, bored, sluggish—or simply exhausted? It's amazing how energy can be revived, and life prolonged, when you work with joy. Coco Chanel was still designing dresses and over-seeing her empire well into her eighties.

Doing the activities she loved kept her feeling young and well. She once said, "There is no time for cut-and-dried monotony. There is time for work. And time for love. That leaves no other time!"

When you don't do what you enjoy your health can suffer. Common signs of neglecting your passion can include, headaches, insomnia, tiredness, depression, and irritability. The body never lies; however, many people soldier on ignoring the obvious warning signs. It's easy to rationalize these feelings away, but the reality is your body is screaming out for something different.

Your Challenge

When you feel unfulfilled or drained of energy what do you notice? How does this differ from times when you are happy?

Work with love—do something that inspires you. Even 15 minutes a day dedicated to passion will boost your energy

Just as appetite comes from eating, so work brings inspiration, if inspiration is not discernible at the beginning

~ Igor Stravinsky, composer

PRINCIPLE SEVEN:

EMPOWER YOUR RELATIONSHIPS

MAINTAIN YOUR INDEPENDENCE

I never wanted to weigh more heavily on a man than a bird

~ Coco Chanel

Whether you work for yourself or with your life partner it's important to maintain your financial and personal independence.

Throughout history this is something that women have fought for and are still fighting for. Equality, reciprocity, and sharing are all important elements of many successful relationships.

Weighing heavily on another person, waiting for a knight in gleaming armor to come and rescue you, or some other fictional notion of living a happily dependent life seldom achieves longevity. Even when the relationship endures, seeds of resentment can fester.

Coco Chanel learned a painful truth in childhood—she could not afford to rely on anyone, certainly, not her father—nor her lovers. Not in the long term.

Not if she was going to achieve the freedom she desired—to become the woman, the person, the success she believed was her destiny.

Boy Capel, the British playboy and industrialist, betrayed her by marrying another woman, although their affair continued until his death in a car crash.

While she was devastated, she wanted to be his equal. His rejection made her even more determined to maintain her financial independence, and the security that being able to fend for herself provided.

However, independence taken too far can have its downsides. Sometimes being emotionally supported by another, and trusting others to care for you when you are in need, is a great comfort.

Interdependence in a relationship can enable you to have the best of both realms.

Your Challenge

How can you maintain your independence?

What would you have to disbelieve about leaning on others that would support you?

How a person masters his fate is more important than what his fate is

~ Wilhelm von Humboldt, philosopher

LIVE WITH OTHERS

One shouldn't live alone. It's a mistake. I used to think I had to make my life on my own, but I was wrong

~ Coco Chanel

While Coco was adept at getting powerful men to support her dreams she was less successful in securing an everlasting commitment. She died aged 87. She was a rich successful woman—but alone.

She once said, "A simple life, with a husband and children—a life with people you love—that is the real life." She also said, "Whatever her age, a woman needs to be looked after by a man who loves her . . . without that look she dies."

Only in her lonely old age did she realize the truth that had eluded her. Perhaps if she had put as much energy into creating a successful intimate relationship as she did building her career she may have died a happier woman with no regrets.

Your Challenge

How can you remain true to yourself while still surrounding yourself with those that love and support you?

A career is wonderful thing, but you can't snuggle up to it on a cold night
~ Marilyn Monroe, actress

FLEE FALSE LOVE

Jump out the window if you are the object of passion. Flee it if you feel it. Passion goes, boredom remains

~ Coco Chanel

Much of Coco's love life was one of affairs. Perhaps she never felt she deserved a committed monogamous relationship with a man she loved.

Or perhaps the wounds of her past followed her like a shadow, making her run from commitment and fearing abandonment.

Whatever her reasons, she knew false love can impede your success, rob your peace of mind, and break your heart

A great relationship is about two things:

1. Finding out the similarities

2. Respecting the differences

No respect, no love. It's hard to respect a married person who has affairs and lies to their spouse. And it's hard to remain in a relationship with someone who doesn't respect your differences and love you for being you

Your Challenge

If the quality of your intimate relationships is causing you stress seek help to clarify the source. Work on your self-esteem if need be

Love yourself more than your need to be in a dysfunctional relationship

Reserve your right to think, for even to think wrongly is better than not to think at all

~ Hypatia of Alexandria

HEAL YOUR WOUNDS

I imposed black; it is still going strong today, for black wipes out everything else around

~ Coco Chanel

As very young children, we're literally 'psychic sponges' actively soaking up the images, emotions, and events in our environment.

If, as it was for Coco Chanel, your childhood was traumatic, the resulting irrational feelings and fears you're left with in adulthood are often buried deep in your subconscious.

Unless brought to the light for healing these buried wounds can exert a negative impact on your relationships, self-esteem and beliefs about the love you need, want and deserve.

Coco craved loved. She yearned to be accepted. She ached to realize the dream that sustained her in the Convent as she devoured illicitly obtained romance novels. That one day she would be the heroine of her own love story and be married happily ever after.

Tragically this never happened for her. Perhaps the truth of the tainted past she fought so hard to keep a secret, caught up with her.

But what if low self-esteem and self-worth prevented her from allowing others to see and love her true vulnerable self?

Your Challenge

Bring to light the wounds of your past. Work with a skilled professional if necessary to bring healing

Forgive those who have trespassed against you—including your parents. The chances are they have unresolved wounds too

Nothing has a stronger influence psychologically on their environment and especially on their children than the unlived life of the parent

~ Carl Jung, psychologist

LET THE CHILDREN PLAY

As long as you know men are like children, you know everything!

~ Coco Chanel

Chanel was the lover of many successful, powerful— and capricious men.

"Women have always been the strong ones of the world. The men are always seeking from women a little pillow to put their heads down on. They are always longing for the mother who held them as infants," she once said.

Her strategy for success was not to take their outbursts, or sudden and unpredictable changes in attitude or behavior seriously—instead she treated them playfully.

"Sometimes you have to suck it up," says Rachel the wife of a very successful, and sometimes highly stressed, chef. "I have to remind myself that it's not about me and just stay relaxed," she once told me.

Men may be childish at times—but we love children don't we! What do children crave? Attention? Cuddles? To be your number one focus? To be left alone? Or just your unconditional love? We need the same things sometimes.

Your Challenge

If you live with an alpha male, or someone with tempestuous moods, or a person with continual demands on your time or energy, consider how you may weather their emotional storms and seemingly incessant needs more playfully

I know now that most people are so closely concerned with themselves that they are not aware of their own individuality, I can see myself, and it has helped me to say what I want to say in paint

~ Georgia O'Keeffe, artist

CONFLICT HAPPENS

It's probably not just by chance that I'm alone. It would be very hard for a man to live with me, unless he's terribly strong. And if he's stronger than I, I'm the one who can't live with him

~ Coco Chanel

While you need others to survive and thrive, success in work and in life is more likely when your relationships are harmonious.

But, as much as we all like to get on, sometimes conflict is inevitable. People may feel threatened by your success, they may deliberately try to thwart you, or they may misunderstand your motives and desires.

Your family and loved ones may resent the time you need to spend away from them. You may feel guilty for wanting more from your life.

You may clash with your business or intimate partners—as Coco did. People may try to rip you off, cheat you, rob you—or leave you. Be prepared—conflict is inevitable, no matter how kind or good-hearted or savvy you feel you are.

As Coco said, "I don't care what you think. I don't think about you at all." Care more about how well you handle conflict when it happens, and plan your conflict-handling strategy appropriately.

Your Challenge

What do others fear? What are their agendas?

How might they want the best for you?

How might they want the worst for you?

Why might your success threaten them?

How sharp are your conflict resolution skills?

How are you unnecessarily or unknowingly creating conflict?

Learn from your experiences

I am a woman in process. I'm just trying like everybody else. I try to take every conflict, every experience, and learn from it. Life is never dull

~ Oprah Winfrey, businesswoman

SHOW YOUR STRENGTH

Gentleness doesn't get work done unless you happen to be a hen laying eggs

~ Coco Chanel

Having healthy boundaries in all of your relationships is key to being productive, healthy and happy. Very often having healthy boundaries requires assertiveness.

The challenge is that many people confuse being assertive with being aggressive. This often leads to passive behavior where people may feel like they aren't being heard, valued or respected.

Issues with boundaries also happen in other kinds of relationships. A common example is a person who works from home and is constantly being interrupted by their family.

If they confuse being assertive with aggression then they may never ask their family to respect their time when they are working.

Whether you think being assertive is unpleasant or fear people won't like you if you show your strength, there'll come a time when you need to show some muscle.

So, what exactly is the difference between being assertive and being aggressive? While the two may look similar from the outside, they are worlds apart.

1. Assertiveness comes from a place of valuing yourself as equal to others.

Rather than valuing yourself less than another person (passive) or valuing yourself more than another person (aggressive), assertiveness means you value yourself equal to others.

For example, in negotiations an assertive person knows that they are looking for a fair exchange of value on all sides. An aggressive person is more concerned with what they can get out of it and may use fear tactics to get what they want.

2. Assertiveness is done with the intention of hurting no one.

Because sometimes people react poorly to assertiveness, then it's easy to see why someone would confuse it with aggression. The truth is that when someone is being assertive they are doing so with the intention of hurting no one, including themselves.

Unfortunately, we can't control how other people react to our own assertiveness, so sometimes being assertive will lead to hurt feelings even if that was never the intention.

3. Assertiveness means you speak to the point.

Assertive people are not afraid to express their opinion and stand up for themselves, even if it won't be liked. In short, being assertive is done from a place of love for all (including oneself), whereas aggression comes from a place of fear.

Coco Chanel had to stand up for herself and her needs on many, many occasions. One of the most infamous examples was her ongoing battle with the brothers she went into partnership with to produce Chanel N°5.

She spent years in protracted, often acrimonious and litigious negotiations to gain a fair share of the profits from the sales of Chanel N°5 from her business partners. Had she been gentle, the chances are she never would have won.

Your Challenge

Be strong—speak up and fight to be respected if need be

Take assertiveness classes if you find yourself passively accepting a less than fair deal

Maintain your boundaries—push back when people breach them

If I was a guy, they would think I'm just opinionated. But as a woman, I'm 'difficult.' I mean, I can't change sex

~ Dame Zaha Mohammad Hadid, architect

PRINCIPLE EIGHT:

EMPOWER YOUR WORK

BE A LOVE MARK

A life with people you love—that is the real life

~ Coco Chanel

Conventional science teaches that the main role of the heart is to pump blood around your body. But that's just a tiny part of its power.

Your heart has an intelligence far greater than your brain. Scientific studies also confirm that your heart has the biggest and most powerful electromagnetic field.

But the heart, like any major organ needs nourishment to perform miracles. Feed and oxygenate your heart with all the things and people you love.

True fervent love is not something you can turn on and off like a tap. It's an obsession so consuming it feeds your soul. It can be as tangible as a vocation, or a house or as intangible as a dream or an idea. You could be in love with anything.

Here's a few of the things Coco loved with a passion:

- ✓ Mysticism
- ✓ A cause
- ✓ Analyzing and understanding things

- ✓ Books
- ✓ Creativity
- ✓ The future
- ✓ Perfume
- ✓ An idea
- ✓ Freedom
- ✓ Independence
- ✓ Interesting and talented men

She created an enduring personal and professional brand through these Love Marks.

Your Challenge

What captures your heart's interest and attention? List as many things as you can that you love passionately

People feed off passions—not professions. Become a 'Love Mark' and magnetize people and opportunities toward you

Maintain the balance—try 'the rocking chair test' . . . what would you regret never having achieved when you reach old age and reflect back on your life?

If there's no love, what then?

~ Leonardo da Vinci, artist

You may want to read more about how to be a Love Mark in my book *Mid-Life Career Rescue: Employ Yourself*—getBook.at/EmployYourself.

FOLLOW YOUR JOY

There is no time for cut-and-dried monotony. There is time for work. And time for love. That leaves no other time!

~ Coco Chanel

"Ask a Leo about the secret of leadership or a successful life and they will invariably list passion and tenacity, and a predisposition towards joy as the proper tools for the job," writes Steven Weiss in his book, *Signs of Success: The Remarkable Power of Business Astrology.*

As a Leo, Coco exemplified this. She knew that you can succeed at almost anything if you follow your joy. This is where you soul meets the road, as a tire meets the asphalt—accelerating you toward your preferred future and fueling your success.

When you tap into your joy, you tap into an unlimited reservoir of energy and enthusiasm.

The French take it further—of course! *Jouissance*, literally means orgasmic joy. It's derived from the word from *jouir* ("to enjoy"). Jouissance is to enjoy something a lot! As we've discussed, one of my favorite creativity experts Mihaly Czikszentmihaly, refers to this as a state of "flow."

In a popular YouTube talk he asks, "What makes a life worth living?" Money cannot make us happy, he says—instead, he urges us to learn from people who find pleasure and lasting satisfaction in activities that bring about the state of transcendent "flow."

Coco Chanel was flowing when she designed her clothes, she was flowing when she attended to the minutest details of her garments. For her, her work had a spiritual aspect. It wasn't a job—it was her métier, or vocation.

I feel this way when I write books like this. I love writing. I would willingly do this activity for free—and often do. This is a sign of flow, according to Czikszentmihaly.

Others signs are the things that come easily or naturally to you—especially when combined with "*jouir*." I often refer to this state of flow as following your passion.

Some of the most common questions I'm asked by people who seeking coaching is, "How can I find out what I'm good at?" and "How can I be sure that I will enjoy it and succeed?"

Whilst these questions may seem daunting, the past is often a good predictor of the future.

Often, we just need reminding of the times and circumstances in our lives when we felt inspired or energized by something, the times when our skills just seemed to flow. These moments can provide clues to our passions, unique strengths and talents.

I feel most in flow when I am creating. I also lose all track of time when I am painting. The most fulfilling part of this is making something that is innately satisfying to me, and that the recipient also truly loves. I feel excited, energized and truly complete.

Sometimes before I sit down to paint, write or create in any way I find it really hard to get going. During such times, I find that Picasso's words of wisdom, "Inspiration exists, but it has to find us working," motivates me into action.

I discipline myself and say I will give it 30 minutes and that's all. Very often I find that three or four later I am blissfully painting and find it hard to tear myself away.

Writing posts and articles that help people to follow their bliss produces the same state. I feel a huge sense of purpose and people comment positively about my flow-inspired works.

I know Coco Chanel felt the same.

Your Challenge

Find something you're passionate about and keep hugely interested in it, by feeding and nurturing your passion every day

Nothing you want is upstream. What comes easily you to you? What is a struggle for you?

Flow has to find you working—take action. Do what you love

Collect examples of people who followed their joy and made a rewarding career and/or enriched their lives

All My life I have been mistaken in measuring the significance of any work by the struggles that went into it

~ Henri Matisse, artist

If you need more help finding and living your life purpose you may wish to read my book, *Find Your Passion and Purpose: Four Easy Steps to Discover a Job You Want and Live the Life You Love*, available as a paperback and eBook from Amazon will help. Navigate to here getBook.at/Passion.

DO THE WORK

*There is time for work. And time
for love. That leaves no other time!*

~ Coco Chanel

If there was one thing Coco Chanel wasn't afraid of it was hard work. Born into poverty she didn't have the luxury of procrastinating, or deluding herself that someday, maybe tomorrow, she would do her greatest work.

It helped, of course, that she loved what she did with such a passion that work didn't feel like work at all.

But even when you love what you do, it can be a struggle to show up and do what you need to do. At times the tasks required to complete your finest work can lie outside your comfort or knowledge zone. Show up anyway.

You may be having a bad hair day. Show up anyway. Perhaps there's some drama going on around you, or you're just plain tired. Show up anyway—even if it's only for five or ten minutes or half an hour. Who knows, you may just find yourself re-inspired.

As Paulo Coelho, author of *The Alchemist*, shared on the Tim Ferris show, "I have the book inside me, I start procrastinating in the morning. I checked my emails, I check news—I check anything that I could check just to avoid the moment to sit and face myself as a writer in front of my book.

"For three hours, I am trying to tell myself, 'No, no, no. Later, later, later.' Then later not to lose face in front of myself I tell myself to sit and write for half an hour, and of course, this half an hour becomes 10 hours in a row.

"That's why I write my books so quickly. Very quickly, because I cannot stop. *I cannot stop.* And then of course at night I take a lot of notes because I am still in the speed of writing the book, the next day these notes are useless.

"The same thing happens again: checking emails, going to social communities, postponing, procrastinating. And this I cannot stop it's my ritual. I have to feel guilty of not writing for three hours or four hours. But then I start writing non-stop. In two weeks I have the book ready."

Your Challenge

Surrender to procrastination—set a time limit and then get on with it!

Or, be a creative procrastinator—put off everything that doesn't advance your dreams

Show up! Show up! When you show up your muse will too! Just like mine did as I wrote this chapter in five

minutes, despite telling myself I would do it tomorrow—
all thanks to James Patterson's quote below!

*Do NOT sit there like 'Oh I don't feel
like it today. I don't feel like it tomorrow'.
Feel like it! Do it! Force yourself*

~ James Patterson, author

TAKE YOUR CHANCE

*A girl should be two things:
who and what she wants*

~ Coco Chanel

In French *chance* means 'luck'. Chanel and Chance sound so similar as if they were created for each other.

Coco Chanel deeply believed in the power of luck. Taking chances and following opportunities defined her—even when there was no guarantee of success.

She believed in harnessing the arbiters of good fortune and the power of dreams and oracles as predictors of future success.

When she was a poor young woman cloistered in a convent orphanage she dreamed of a romantic life, and fueled her dreams of happily-ever-after with romantic novels she read again and again.

When the chance came to live the life she had imagined she grabbed it—aligning herself with wealthy men who could provide the life she wanted. So, it's no surprise that one of her most popular and enduing perfumes is named '*Chance.*'

"Unexpected. Unpredictable. Irresistible. Delicately sparkling, endlessly romantic, vibrant, fresh and

spirited," are just some of the words used to describe this popular perfume—it's not chance that they also define the woman behind the brand.

Upon Coco's death, a pack of Tarot cards was discovered in her apartment. The number five, which was her lucky number, was on top. A collection of symbolic objects was scattered throughout her room.

She looked for signs and symbols in the ordinary, a spray of roses, a pure white camellia, a Catholic icon, and she also believed in theosophy. All of which boosted her belief in the power of chance and bolstered her confidence in taking inspiring action.

Your Challenge

What irresistible idea or opportunity could you take a chance on?

What signs, symbols or spiritual practice could you harness to boost your confidence?

Success is defined by the things you say yes to. What makes you happy?

Women are always told, 'You're not going to make it, it's too difficult, you can't do that, don't enter this competition, you'll never win it.' They need confidence in themselves and people around them to help them to get on

~ Dame Zaha Mohammad Hadid, architect

BE ORIGINAL

*In order to be irreplaceable
one must always be different*

~ Coco Chanel

Coco's commitment to reinventing herself in order to remain true to her essence at any cost is the reason why her name and her brand have persisted.

The Chanel brand might have ended with the death in the 1970's of this complex woman who founded the businesses that carried her name, and quietly disappeared from our cultural imagination.

Instead, both Coco Chanel and Chanel the business have proven astonishingly resilient. Originality, authenticity and reinvention was a crucial part of Chanel's success.

Your power to choose the focus of your life allows you to reinvent yourself, to change your future, and to powerfully influence the rest of your life—something Coco knew very well.

"I invented my life by taking for granted that everything I did not like would have an opposite, which I would like," Coco once said. Coco also said, "Hard times arouse an instinctive desire for authenticity."

Your Challenge

Whether you're bored, stressed, anxious or under economic attack, adapt to changing circumstances—reinvent your career and your life

A big part of originality is following your own truth. If you think something is a great idea—try it. Don't get bogged down by fear, or subscribing to other people's ideas and taking their work as your standard

Be a trailblazer like all the great inventors, and have the satisfaction of being authentically you. Determine who you are and who you choose to be

Create a life or work of heart that is as original as you are. Believe in your capacity for originality

Take your opinion as your standard. Bring forth your passion and infuse your life and work with your true essence—all else will follow

There will come a time when you believe everything is finished. That will be the beginning

~ Louis L'Amour, novelist

KNOW WHEN TO CHANGE

*Don't spend time beating on a wall,
hoping to transform it into a door*

~ Coco Chanel

To keep opportunities flowing you need to respond to signs that it's time to open new doors. Your intuitive guidance, body barometer and willingness to reach beyond your current limitations, real or imagined, can be a game-changer.

Living this way requires daring and playful leaps outside of your comfort zone, and moment-by-moment navigation. Even a small detour and following your curiosity can have a beneficial impact.

Coco Chanel expertly blended intuitive instinct with an acute awareness of the forces that shaped demand for her products. The looming war guided her designs toward more practical, masculine lines and durable fabrics.

Women's cry for liberation from constraint inspired trousers and business suits, and the need to diversify her product range motivated her to go in search of creating a perfume.

She was the consummate Renaissance woman—reinventing herself numerous times, she is one of the early adopters of what I call a "Career Combo"— threading different business activities throughout her career. Her ability to shape-shift enabled Coco to quickly adapt to changing fortunes.

For many successful people having several skills or jobs is the best way to manage unpredictable or unsustainable cash flow—and to finance a desired change of career.

For example, DJ Lemon is passionate about music. However, his love for reggae doesn't pay well, so he continues to combine his passion for music with working as a barber. Shelly is training to be a movie director, but knows she can fall back on her nursing skills when work is thin.

Your Challenge

How can you tune into your instincts and heed the call for change? Could you do a career combo?

What or who could support you to step outside of your comfort zone? What new doors, or new worlds would you like to break into? How will you feel when you have succeeded?

What the caterpillar calls the end of the world, the master calls the butterfly

~ Richard Bach, author

JEALOUS SABOTEURS

*I don't care what you think about me.
I don't think about you at all*

~ Coco Chanel

Chanel's confidence, some say arrogance, was hard won. She'd worked her way up from literally nothing to become one of the most popular designers in the history of fashion. But with the coming of World War II, her fame would turn into infamy.

During the war, Chanel became mired in controversy. When the Nazis marched on Paris, Chanel responded by shutting down her business and becoming involved with Hans Gunther von Dincklage, a Nazi officer 13 years her junior. In return, von Dincklage allowed Chanel to continue to reside in her beloved Ritz Hotel.

Was Coco the Mata Hari of the fashion world? Alternately the toast and scourge of Paris, Coco Chanel's reputation never fully recovered from her affair with this Nazi intelligence officer during World War II. But according to one historian, Chanel may have been more of a war hero than a war criminal.

Edmonde Charles-Roux, considered the most reliable of Chanel's biographers, has offered circumstantial but credible evidence that Chanel was sent by Walter

Schellenberg, a ranking officer in German intelligence, on a peace mission to British prime minister Winston Churchill. Schellenberg was reportedly acting on behalf of Gestapo leader Heinrich Himmler, who attempted to offer secret peace initiatives to the Allies toward the end of the war.

Rumors surrounding this period abound. Coco is lucky she escaped with her life. Others weren't so lucky. Mata Hari, an exotic dancer and high class courtesan, seven years Coco's senior, was executed in her 40's for similar 'crimes'—loving men regardless of nationality, and as a result being accused of treason. Chanel called in favors from the powerful men in her life, favors Mata Hari also tried to call in—to no avail.

After the liberation of France, French resistance forces arrested Chanel for her wartime activities. But Churchill, a close friend of one of Chanel's former lovers, the Duke of Westminster, is said to have intervened on her behalf. Chanel was released just 24 hours after her arrest and immediately left France for Switzerland, where she is buried.

Was Coco a spy? I doubt it. Was she a survivor? Undoubtedly. And does any of it really matter now? Westerners are now bedfellows of the Russians, Japanese, and Germans—all those 'enemies' people fought and died for—men and women with hearts and dreams and a wish for peace, just as she did.

Your Challenge

Others may be jealous or critical of your success—succeed anyway!

Wage war on your enemy. Shoot down your saboteurs with your nonchalance

I had another dream the other day about music critics. They were small and rodent-like with padlocked ears, as if they had stepped out of a painting by Goya

~ Igor Stravinsky, composer

GIVE GENEROUSLY

*Hard times arouse an instinctive
desire for authenticity*

~ Coco Chanel

It's a myth that only the mean and cruel amass success. Born in a poor house, and raised in a convent founded by the saintly Étienne, a man renowned for his gifts of charity, Coco Chanel experienced first-hand the blessings of those who gave generously to those in need.

Throughout her life she returned these blessings to others, including financially supporting the struggling composer Igor Stravinsky, impoverished exiled Tzars, and fallen Russian aristocracy to whom she gave employment.

Raised by the Church she would have been familiar with St Nicholas and his legendary generosity which led him to be called 'Santa Claus' and become a patron saint of children and the needy.

One of the most famous stories about him describes his rescue of three young girls whose father was about to send them into prostitution to save the impoverished family. The saint threw three bags of gold through the girls' bedroom window so that their future was secure.

When you contribute with joy and give to others from the spirit of love, and are totally detached from the outcome of your offering, you'll be surprised at how the Universe gives back to you.

Your Challenge

The more you give, the more you receive. Start or continue giving time, money, assistance, or goods to those in need. This will help affirm how much you have, and lead to larger feelings of abundance. This automatically attracts greater prosperity into your life

Call upon St Nicholas to inspire and guide your volunteer work and show you the best avenues to give donations

Keep a gratitude journal and give thanks daily for everything you are grateful for.

List some ways you could pay your good fortune forward. It may be as simple as telling someone how much you appreciate them

There is some strange alchemy associated with gratitude. Somewhere along the way of doing these lists, I fell in love with my life again

~ Anne Dowsett Johnston, author and recovering alcoholic

CONCLUSION:
BEAUTY AND THE BEST

"The heavens often rained down the richest gifts on human beings, naturally, but sometimes with lavish abundance bestow upon a single individual beauty, grace and ability, so that, whatever he does, every action is so divine that he distances all other men, and clearly displays how his genius is the gift of God and not an acquirement of human art."

~ Giorgio Vasari, in *The Lives of The Artists*

The belief in power of beauty was central to everything Coco Chanel pursued. Inspired by astrology, tarot, numerology, theosophy and the divine healing power of the plant world, she knew that nature and spirituality held the immortal secrets of both beauty and power.

"Fashion has two purposes: comfort and love. Beauty comes when fashion succeeds," she once said.

While Coco is arguably most famous as a designer, she was the archetype of a Renaissance woman. Her unquenchable zest for life was equaled only by the power of her determination, vision and aptitude for creation.

Beauty is timeless, holding sacred universal wisdom and truth. The artist Paul Klee once said, 'One eye sees and the other feels'. And this ability to touch our souls is where Coco Chanel has surpassed many others.

Beauty and Your Success

Beauty comes from the inside. It's your essence—so authentic that, just as there will never be another Coco, there will never be another you.

The art of success lies in bringing more beauty into this world. It lies in being you. It's a secret that ancient masters and philosophers understood well. And it's a secret that modern day successful people also know and harness.

Businessmen and women, politicians, and the most successful artists understand that intrinsic, authentic, soulful beauty attracts. Beauty is irresistible. Beauty sells.

You may not be aiming to create the next acclaimed perfume, but if you infuse your life and work with your energy, power, talent and essence, who knows—100 years from today somebody may well be writing a book about you and the legacy you left.

You may think the outcome has to happen in a certain way, on a certain day, to reach your goal. But human willpower cannot make everything happen. Spirit has its own idea, of how the arrow flies, and upon what wind it travels.

It may not happen overnight, but if you follow your heart, maintain your focus, and take inspired action your time will come.

I promise!

If by some strange twist of fate, it doesn't? At least you'll know you tried. A life of no regrets—now that's worth striving for.

Let the beauty you love be the life that you live. Now go out and create great art!

THE TRUTH ABOUT SUCCESS

*Every day is a fashion show
and the world is the runway*

~ Coco Chanel

I've distilled Coco's principles for success down to twenty-one facts—or TRUTHS as I call them. And the wonderful thing is that these truths can be embodied by you. You can be, have and do whatever your heart desires if you're determined to succeed and look for ways to put these truths into practice.

1 Love

2 Talent

#3 Curiosity

#4 Learning

#5 Interest

#6 Vision

7 Service/Purpose

8 Opportunity

#9 Focus

#10 Commitment

#11 Values

#12 Motivation

#13 Labor

#14 Asking/accepting help

#15 Goals

#16 Optimism

#17 Virtue/Integrity

#I18 Instinct

#19 Strength

#20 Energy

#21 Determination

I know you can succeed at whatever you set your heart, mind and soul to. Pursue your liberty—be free to be you. Have the courage and confidence to define success on your own terms.

Follow your passions, cultivate your natural and dormant talents, remain curious and embrace learning, follow your interests, maintain your vision, work with purpose and be of service.

When opportunity knocks, open the door. If it doesn't knock, go out and create opportunities. Focus on what you desire, not what you fear. Commit—devote yourself to your quest for success.

Let your values guide you—they are your truth-compass. Clarify what motivates you, be this extrinsic or intrinsic rewards. Do the work—no matter how small the effort. In time you will amass success.

Ask your way to success, and learn from those with the skill, knowledge and power to help you. Don't be shy, proud or nervous to ask for help!

Set goals—little, bigger and bigger still. Stretch and grow and strive to make the impossible possible. Celebrate your successes along the way—no matter how small.

Cultivate optimism—water it regularly and never let faith and hope wither from neglect.

Maintain your integrity and virtue. Follow your hunches, intuition and instinct. Be grateful for all that you have—be it health, friends, support, or your cat.

Maximize your energy—look after your mind, body and soul. And lastly, but perhaps also firstly, play. Alleviate the pressure—don't take yourself too seriously.

Be joyful in success—and also while attempting success. Keep your feet on the ground, your head in the clouds and ride the magic carpet of your creative imagination.

But most of all, 'do a Coco'—stand out from the crowd and dare to be different, even if others think you're crazy!

Imperfection is beauty, madness is genuis and it's better to be absolutely ridiculous than absolutely boring

~ Marilyn Monroe, actress

The two men I've loved, I think, will remember me, on earth or in heaven, because men always remember a woman who caused them concern and uneasiness. I've done my best, in regard to people and to life, without precepts, but with a taste for justice

~ Coco Chanel

ALSO BY CASSANDRA GAISFORD

Mid-Life Career Rescue: The Call for Change

Take the stress out of making a change, confirm your best-fit career and move toward your preferred future.

#1 Amazon Best-Seller. Available in print and eBook from Amazon—getBook.at/CareerChange

Mid-Life Career Rescue: What Makes You Happy

Clarify what makes you happy and find your point of brilliance.

#1 Amazon Best-Seller. Available in print and eBook—getBook.at/MakeYouHappy

Mid-Life Career Rescue: Employ Yourself

Start a business on the side while holding down your job. Or take the leap to self-employed bliss. Choose and grow your own business with confidence. This handy resource will show you how.

#1 Amazon Best-Seller. Available in print and eBook—getBook.at/EmployYourself

Mid-Life Career Rescue
-Three Book Bundle-

Box Set (Books 1-3): *The Call for Change, What Makes You Happy, Employ Yourself*

More passion, less career groundhog day! Fast-Track your success and instantly save $$$ when you buy this bundle of 3 eBook Amazon best-sellers.

Available for immediate download— getBook.at/CareerRescueBox

Find Your Passion and Purpose

Focus your energy and time to achieve outstanding personal and professional results. Find your point of brilliance and purpose in life.

#1 Amazon Best-Seller. Available in print and eBook from Amazon—getBook.at/Passion

Boost Your Self-Esteem and Confidence

Be empowered! Heed the call for greater self-confidence, self-esteem, self-value and love you more. Six easy steps to increase self-confidence, self-esteem, self-value and love yourself more

Available in print and eBook from Amazon— getBook.at/BoostYourSelfEsteemAndConfidence

The Art of Success: Leonardo Da Vinci

The 8-Step Blueprint to True Success for Your Relationships, Your Bank Account, Your Body and Your Soul

Leonardo da Vinci had to overcome obstacles to success just like you and I. Be inspired by his blueprint for success.

Available in print and eBook from Amazon— getBook.at/TheArtofSuccess

More of Cassandra's practical and inspiring workbooks on a range of career and life enhancing topics can be found on her Amazon Author Page.

Navigate to: Author.to/CassandraGaisford

FURTHER RESOURCES

E-BOOKS

More of Cassandra's practical and inspiring workbooks on a range of career and life enhancing topics can be found on her Amazon Author Page. Navigate to: https://www.amazon.com/Cassandra-Gaisford

NEWSLETTERS

For inspiring tools and helpful tips subscribe to Cassandra's free newsletters here: http://www.worklifesolutions.nz/home

Sign up now and receive a free eBook!

SURF THE NET

www.whatthebleep.com—a powerful and inspiring site emphasizing quantum physics and the transformational power of thought.

www.heartmath.org—comprehensive information and tools help you access your intuitive insight and heart based knowledge. Validated and supported by science-based research. Check out the additional information about your heart-brain.

www.personalitytype.com—created by the authors of *Do What You Are: Discover the Perfect Career for You through the Secrets of Personality Type*. This site focuses on expanding your awareness of your own type and that of others—including children and partners. This site also contains many useful links.

Join polymath Tim Ferris and learn from his interesting and informative guests on The Tim Ferris Show http://fourhourworkweek.com/podcast/

BOOKS

Celebrate being an outlier and learn why clocking up 10,000 hours will help you succeed in Malcolm Gladwell's *Outliers: The Story of Success.*

Struggling in an extroverted world? Introverts are enjoying a renaissance, fueled in part by Susan Cain's terrific bestseller Quiet: The Power of Introverts in a World That Can't Stop Talking

Copy-cat your way to success with Austin Kleon's great book, *Steal Like an Artist.*

Learn more about Chanel's fascinating life in Justine Picardie's excellent books, *The Secret Life of Coco Chanel* and Coco Chanel: *The Legend and The Life*

Discover more about the creation and battle for supremacy of Chanel's perfume empire in, *The Secret of Chanel No. 5: The Intimate History of the World's Most Famous Perfume,* by Tilar Mazzeo.

Learn more about scientific prayer therapy and other ways to program your mind for success in Joseph Murphy's (PhD.) excellent book, *The Miracle of Mind Dynamics.*

FOLLOW ME AND CONTINUE TO BE INSPIRED

www.facebook.com/cassandra.gaisford
http://twitter.com/cassandraNZ
www.pinterest.com/worklifenz
www.youtube.com/user/cassandragaisfordnz

BLOG

Learn more about happiness at work and life by visiting my either of my two blogs:

https://powerfulcreativity.wordpress.com.   You'll find a variety of tips and inspiration to help you tip into the power of creativity—personally and professionally.

http://www.worklifesolutions.nz/category/latest. You'll find a variety of articles and tips about people pursuing their passion and strategies to help you pursue yours.

PRESENTATIONS

For information about products and workshops navigate to here http://www.cassandragaisford.com/contact/spea king To ask Cassandra to come and speak at your workplace or conference, contact: cassandra@cassandragaisford.com

GRATITUDES

Thank you to Coco Chanel for inspiring me, and to all the other authors and Coco experts who have shared their knowledge, and from whom I gained inspiration as I wrote this book.

To all the wonderful people who took *The Art of Success Questionnaire*. Thank you for your honesty. Your responses were inspiring. Your worries, concerns, dreams and aspirations helped shape this book.

Thank you to all the advance readers—your cheerleading and constructive feedback definitely made this book more successful.

To all the many clients I have helped over the last twenty years—you have brought me joy, fueled my passion and helped me achieve my own inner motivation. Special thanks to Pauline Roberts and Catherine Sloan for being some of my biggest supporters.

To all my friends, for helping me through the emotional obstacle course of writing a book, thank you.

Cate Walker, thanks once again for your fabulous proof-reading and editing. I know it's hard to pick up everything! Coralie Urwin, your accurate eyes and fact checking skills are amazing.

To my authorpreneur tribe, including the uber generous Barry Watson, I'm so blessed to have met so many fruitful collaborators.

And to the love of my life—Laurie Wills, my Templar Knight. Thank you for believing in me. Without your faith, support, commitment, inspiration, and love, I could never have written this book.

AND NOW . . .

Thank you—for purchasing and reading my books. You are more than my livelihood: you let me live my passion. Without your enthusiasm, desire and courage, the ideas in this book would never have flourished. I hope you enjoyed *The Art of Success* and that you'll be encouraged to follow your path with heart. Dare to be different—your uniqueness is truly your greatest gift.

Thank you for trusting me to guide you. I really hope you loved this book as much as I truly enjoyed writing it. And I hope it aids your success, as I have succeeded and flourished during the many hours I spent writing *The Art of Success.* Here's to an extra-ordinary level of happiness and success in all our lives.

With love,

PLEASE LEAVE A REVIEW

Your feedback encourages and sustains me and I love hearing from you.

Show your support. Share how this book has helped you by leaving a REVIEW ON AMAZON—Even a one-liner would be helpful.

I recently received an email from a reader who said, "Your books are a fantastic resource and until now I never even thought to write a review. Going forward I will be reviewing more books. So many great ones out there and I want to support the amazing people that write them."

Great reviews also help people find good books.

Leave a REVIEW ON AMAZON— getBook.at/CocoChanel

PS: If you enjoyed this book, do me a small favour to help spread the word about it and share the *Art of Success page* on Facebook, Twitter and other social networks.

www.worklifesolutions.nz/books/the-art-of-success/

ABOUT THE AUTHOR

Cassandra Gaisford is an award-winning artist, #1 Amazon best-selling author, and holistic energy psychologist. A corporate escapee, she now lives and works from her idyllic lifestyle property overlooking the Bay of Islands in New Zealand.

Cassandra is also an aspiring author of historical art-related fiction. She loves all the arts, traveling, orchids and anything that is inspiring, uplifting and beautiful.

FOLLOW CASSANDRA AND CONTINUE TO BE INSPIRED

www.cassandragaisford.com
www.twitter.com/gethappyatwork
www.instagram.com/midlife_career_rescue
www.facebook.com/worklifesolutions

www.pinterest.com/worklifenz
www.youtube.com/user/cassandragaisfordnz

Made in the USA
San Bernardino, CA
23 August 2017